Hitler's Revenge Weapons

This book is dedicated to my Dutch wife, Margaretha, who endured the Nazi occupation in a part of Holland from which Hitler's revenge weapons were launched, and whose help has been invaluable.

By the same author

Seek and Strike: RAF Brüggen in War and Peace (Astonbridge Publishing, Gloucester, 2001)

Swift Justice: The Supermarine Low Level Reconnaissance Fighter, Pen & Sword Books, Barnsley, 2004

Best of Breed: The Hunter in Fighter Reconnaissance: An Operational History of the Hawker Hunter FR10, Pen & Sword Books, Barnsley, 2006

Voodoo Warriors: The Story of the McDonnell Voodoo Fast Jets, Pen & Sword Books, Barnsley, 2007

Dragon Rampant: The Story of No.234 Fighter Squadron, Merlin Massara Publications, Dunstable, 2007

Built to Endure: The RAF Airfield Construction Branch in the Cold War, Old Forge Publishing, Peterborough, 2009

From the Cockpit No.14: Swift, Ad Hoc Publications, Suffolk, 2011

Thinking the Unthinkable: The Lives of RAF and East German Fast-jet Pilots in the Cold War, Astonbridge Publishing, Gloucester, 2012

Hitler's Revenge Weapons

The Final Blitz of London

Nigel Walpole

Pen & Sword
AVIATION

First published in Great Britain in 2018 by
PEN AND SWORD AVIATION
an imprint of
Pen and Sword Books Ltd
47 Church Street
Barnsley
South Yorkshire S70 2AS

ISBN 978 1 52672 288 1

Printed and bound in the UK
by T J International, Padstow, Cornwall, PL28 8RW

Typeset in Times New Roman 11/13.5 by
Aura Technology and Software Services, India

Pen & Sword Books Ltd incorporates the imprints of Pen & Sword
Archaeology, Atlas, Aviation, Battleground, Discovery,
Family History, History, Maritime, Military, Naval, Politics, Railways,
Select, Social History, Transport, True Crime, Claymore Press,
Frontline Books, Leo Cooper, Praetorian Press, Remember When,
Seaforth Publishing and Wharncliffe.

For a complete list of Pen and Sword titles please contact
Pen and Sword Books Limited
47 Church Street, Barnsley, South Yorkshire, S70 2AS, England
E-mail: enquiries@pen-and-sword.co.uk
Website: www.pen-and-sword.co.uk

Contents

Glossary

AA	Anti-Aircraft
AAEF	Allied Air Expeditionary Force
ADGB	Air Defence of Great Britain
AFS	Auxiliary Fire Service
AIS	American Interplanetary Society
ARP	Air Raid Precautions
AVKO	*Altenwalde Versuchskommando*
CIU	Central Interpretation Unit
FR	Fighter (armed) Reconnaissance
GC & CS	Government Code & Cypher Service
GDA	Gun Defended Area
HTM	*Historisch Technisches Museum*
HVA	*Heeresversuchsanstal*
HWA	*Herres Waffenamt*
JIC	Joint Intelligence Committee
LAA	Light Anti- Aircraft (artillery)
MI15	Military Intelligence Section 15
NII-1	Russian Research Institute
OKW	*Oberkommando der Wehrmacht*
OKH	*Oberkommando der Heeres*
PDU	Photo Development Unit
PGM	Precision Guided Missile
PI	Photographic Interpreter
PIU	Photographic Interpretation Unit
PoW	Prisoner of War
PR	Photographic Reconnaissance
PRU	Photographic Reconnaissance Unit
RAE	Royal Aircraft Establishment
RATO	Rocket Assisted Take-Off
RMB	*Rheinmetall Borsig*

ROC	Royal Observer Corps
SHAEF	Supreme Headquarters Allied Expeditionary Force
SAM	Surface-to-air Missile
SPOG	Special Projectile Operations Group
SS	*Schutzstaffel*
SSM	Surface-to-surface Missile
USSR	Union of Soviet Socialist Republics
VfR	*Verein für Raketen Raumschiffahrt*
WaA	*Herreswaffenamt*
We Prüf	*Heereswaffenamt Prüfwesen*
2TAF	Second Tactical Air Force (RAF)

Equivalent Ranks

Wehrmacht	British Army	Royal Air Force	Schultzstaffel (SS)
Leutnant	Second Lieutenant (Lt)	Pilot Officer (Plt Off)	Untersturmführer
Oberleutnant	Lieutenant (Lt)	Flying Officer (Fg Off)	Obersturmführer
Hauptman	Captain (Capt.)	Flight Lieutenant (Flt Lt)	Hauptsturmführer
Major (Maj)	Major (Maj.)	Squadron Leader (Sqn Ldr)	Sturmbannführer
Oberst Leutnant	Lieutenant Colonel (Lt Col)	Wing Commander (Wg Cdr)	Oberbannführer
Oberst	Colonel (Col)	Group Captain (Gp Capt)	Standartenführer
	Brigadier (Brig.)	Air Commodore (Air Cdre)	Oberführer
Generalmajor	Major General (Maj. Gen.)	Air Vice-Marshal (AVM)	Brigadeführer
Generalleutnant	Lieutenant General (Lt Gen)	Air Marshal (AM)	Gruppenführer
General	General (Gen)	Air Chief Marshal (ACM)	Obergruppenführer
Generaloberst	General (Gen)		Oberstgruppenführer
Generalfeldmarschall	Field Marshal (FM)	Marshal of the RAF (MRAF)	Reichsführer-SS

Preface

From our rowing boat on Connaught Waters, Epping Forest, my sister and I merely glanced up as another of Hitler's first generation *Vergeltungswaffen,* his retaliation or 'revenge' weapons, the V1 flying bomb, 'Doodlebug' or 'buzz-bomb', passed overhead with that ominous, pulsating sound. It was August 1944, and in the previous two months this had become such a familiar sight and sound that it barely deserved comment, except that this one seemed to be heading directly across the Lea Valley to our home when the engine stopped and an eerie silence preceded the inevitable, shattering explosion. There being no telephones immediately available in those days, we hoped for the best, determined to use every minute of the one hour on the water, bought for a precious two shillings (10p). In fact, the tiny, pilotless aircraft did end its days, and those of its victims, in our hometown of Cheshunt, happily missing our house, as would many more in the six months to come. Many of us, particularly those who lived in 'Doodlebug Alley' did become a little blasé with the seemingly endless succession of V1s, unaffected by darkness or bad weather, only diving for the nearest cover, perhaps under a bed or kitchen table, if the engine stopped. For those who were on the receiving end, it was different matter, often a horrific, life changing experience – or worse.

There was no such escape from the second *Vergeltungswaffe,* the V2 stratospheric rocket. Once launched from its site on the continent, again more than 100 miles from London, it became all but invisible to the human eye and gave no warning before impact and penetration, the characteristic double boom following split seconds after ending its supersonic, vertical dive. Short of living fulltime in deep, concrete bunkers, survival from the V2s was a matter of luck, and stoic Londoners became quite fatalistic over their chances.

Luckily, I managed to dodge all the V1s and V2s which landed around me, and I was too young then to appreciate the massive leap forward in the science and engineering the *Vergeltungwaffen* represented. It was only later,

PREFACE

when aeronautics became my profession, that I began to take a real interest in their evolution, gestation and employment, together with the politico-military intrigue which dogged their development, but also the Allies' defences against them. Many erudite texts have dealt with this epic story, some limited to specific aspects, perhaps leaving the reader without the benefit of the necessary background, while others have attempted to cover the whole history, from start to finish, with the danger that the reader might become mired in detail. I have attempted to tell the full story in a relatively short work, of necessity forfeiting some detail in favour of the salient points and particular areas which I hope will be of interest to a lay readership.

Acknowledgements

This account of *Vergeltungswaffen,* Hitler's 'vengeance' weapons, could not have been written without help from those dedicated to these specific aspects of Second World War heritage. In particular, I would like to thank Herr Michael Gericke, and the staff of the *Historisch-Technisches Museum* (HTM), Peenemünde, the staff at Mittelbau-Dora, Valerie Noel at Mimoyecques, the staff at la Coupole and Blockhaus d'Éperlecques, for their assistance and for allowing me to use my camera in their respective museums. I am grateful to Michael Mugford and Chris Halsall for giving me access to the Medmenham Collection and permission to use some photographic reproductions; to Janet Grove of the Waltham Abbey Historical Society; and to local historian, the late Peter Rooke, who helped me recall the effects the flying bombs and rockets had on our young lives in Cheshunt, Hertfordshire. Inevitably, with the number of sources researched, I have found variations in 'fact', detail and, of course, opinion; these have been subject to correlation, interpolation and reservation, and in this I seek the reader's indulgence. To the best of my knowledge, I have not intruded on any intellectual property rights, or used material which is under copyright.

Chapter 1

The Lure of Space

Folklore, if not fact, invariably attributes the introduction of rocketry to the Chinese, based on the belief that, as early as 200 BC, they stumbled on the explosive effects of a 'black powder' – a mixture of saltpetre, sulphur and charcoal – which would be called 'gunpowder'. What is certain is that the Chinese were obsessed with firecrackers and then fireworks, as means of warding off evil spirits. It could also be that the use of this black powder as a propellant was discovered, almost incidentally, when a humble firecracker maker closed one end of a tube filled with the crude explosive, and ignited the other, to have it dart around him erratically until the mixture was exhausted. Be that as it may, it was this principle that would result in the 'rocket', although the term itself was probably not used officially until the fourteenth century. Deeper study reveals a convoluted history, steeped in mythology and legend, told in stories ranging from the outrageous to the believable, with associated dates also arguable.

For instance, it is said that, in about 400 BC, the Greek inventor Archytas heated water in a clay model of a pigeon to boiling point, whereupon it propelled itself along a wire by steam, using the principle of 'action-reaction'. This was copied centuries later by another Greek, Heron Alexandrinus, known as 'Hero of Alexandria', who used steam-propulsion to rotate his aeolipile sphere, to what specific purpose remains unclear. Then there is the tale of man's first known attempt to achieve a vertical take-off in a rocket-borne vehicle, when the Chinese inventor, Wan-Hoo, attached forty-seven rockets to his large wicker chair and had them all ignited simultaneously, he and his chair then vanishing in a puff of smoke – never to be seen again. While continuing to use explosive mixtures in firecrackers and fireworks for displays, the Chinese soon realised the potential of rockets as weapons of war, and in the thirteenth century they began supplementing their traditional bows and arrows with small rockets attached to 'fire arrows', for use against the Mongols in 1232 at the Battle of Kai-fung-fu. Their effectiveness may

1

perhaps be judged by the fact that the Mongols themselves then began developing the rocket for military use.

For most of the next three centuries there was a proliferation of interest in explosive-propelled weapons, including an extraordinary, surface-hugging torpedo, which resembled a giant turtle, designed by the Italian Joanes de Fontana. Meanwhile, the Frenchman Jean Froissart was achieving greater accuracy with rockets fired from tubes, and an English monk, Roger Bacon, increased their range significantly with much improved gunpowder. Towards the end of the sixteenth century, just when enthusiasm for the science seemed to be waning, the German scientist Johann Schmidlap paved the way for space exploration when his modular, two-stage 'step' rocket achieved unprecedented heights.

A century later, in 1687, Sir Isaac Newton put rocket science on a firm footing with his *Philosophiae Naturalis Principia Mathamatica* (*Mathematical Principles of Natural Philosophy*), which established the 'Universal Laws of Motion'. Best known and well proven is his Third Law of Motion': 'For every action there is an equal and opposite reaction'; in effect: 'reaction-thrust', the basic principle of rocket propulsion.

By the end of the eighteenth century, rockets were again gaining some prominence in battle, typically with their use by the Mysore Indians against the British East India Company in southern India. This inspired the British inventor and artillery pioneer Sir William Congreve to develop rockets for use against Napoleon in 1812. Given their lack of accuracy *vis à vis* the gun they tended to be used more in large salvoes, as area weapons, *inter alia* severely affecting the morale of an enemy. While rocket accuracies did improve incrementally, typically with 'spin stabilisation', in which exhaust gasses played on suitably angled vanes, this was outweighed by the development of the breech-loaded cannon and rifled barrels, thus tending to render the gun the battlefield weapon of choice.

Schmidlap's two-stage rocket probably got great minds to think more about the use of rockets in space exploration and they were further encouraged to do so in 1903 by Konstantin Tsiolkovski's visionary reports on the possible use of liquid propellants to achieve the necessary ranges, this earning the Russian the title 'father of modern astronautics'. A little later the American Robert Goddard, while experimenting with forms of propulsion, claimed that, notwithstanding the need for fuel tanks, combustion chambers and turbines, liquid fuels would be the preferred option for space rockets and set out to prove it. His first attempts to do so, using a mixture of petrol and liquid oxygen, sent his rocket a mere forty feet into the air, for a distance of sixty yards in a flight lasting two-and-a-half seconds, but his persistence paid off, as he ventured into gyroscopic control and guidance with ever larger rockets, while developing highly desirable parachute recovery systems.

Meanwhile, Europe was fielding more of its own rocket pioneers. Hermann Oberth, born in Transylvania in 1894, became renowned for his thesis on rocket travel into outer space, *Die Rakete zu den Planetenräumen* (*By Rocket into Planetary Space*), published in 1923. The timing was good; Germany was now rising from the ashes of the First World War, determined to resume what it considered to be its rightful place in the new world, and space was as yet a largely untapped field for exploration. In 1925 Dr Walter Hohmann published *Die Erreichbarkeit der Himmelskörper* (*Reaching the Heavenly Bodies*), which explored orbital dynamics in space and predicted a fuel-efficient path between two different orbits. Suitably impressed, another eminent space writer, Willi Ley, sought Hohmann's help in preparing a selection of papers on the possibility of spaceflight, *Die Möglichkeit der Weltraumfahrt* (*The Possibility of Space Travel*), published in 1928. The successful Apollo landings on the moon and the innovative Voyager spacecraft owe much to Hohmann, who had been able to steer clear of the burgeoning Nazi party and its ambitions for rockets as weapons of war.

Another prominent engineer and science writer of the time, Max Valier, was inspired by Oberth to simplify his mentor's writings for the informed layman in his *Der Vorstoss in der Weltenraum* (*The Advance into Space*), and followed this with several equally worthy articles on the subject – typically 'Berlin to New York in One Hour', and 'A Daring Trip to Mars'. In March 1928 Valier was involved with Friedrich Sander in the successful introduction of the first manned rocket car, the RAK-1, produced by the car maker Fritz von Opel, which achieved a speed of 47 mph, while its successor RAK-2, powered by twenty-four solid-fuel rockets, reached 143 mph. There followed a less successful venture involving a rocket-propelled sailplane named the *Lippisch RRG Raketen-Ente* (Rocket Duck). Fritz Stamer flew this for one mile on its maiden flight but crashed on the second, bringing the whole project to an end. Publicity stunts these may have been, but they all helped to keep the interest in rockets alive.

The *Verein für Raketen Raumschiffahrt* or 'VfR' (Society for Space Travel), established in 1927, may have been the first official forum on space and rocket research. The Society was founded by the rocket scientist

Johannes Winkler, with other prominent pioneers including Oberth, Hohmann, Rudolf Nebel and Willy Ley, and other aspiring rocketeers being among its 500 members. While worthy followers from other nations were accepted, the Germans were very much in charge, interest in the science having spread rapidly throughout Germany. Winkler, and later Ley, edited the society's magazine *Die Rakete* (*The Rocket*).

All this was 'grist to the mill' for the nation's passionate filmgoers, who had become obsessed with science fiction, and this prompted the film producer Fritz Lang to make a film about space travel, *Frau im Mond* (*The Woman on the Moon*). Anticipating an opportunity to obtain funding for their cause, Oberth and Ley offered to build and launch a liquid-fuelled rocket to coincide with the film's first screening and found an ideal setting for this potentially spectacular overture on the Baltic island of Greifswalder Oie, perhaps presaging the subsequent use of nearby Peenemünde for rocket development. Sadly, their rocket suffered many setbacks, with various degrees of damage and injury attributed to the explosive mixtures. In the end the film went ahead one autumn evening in 1929, without the rocket, at Berlin's huge Universal Film AG (UFA) cinema, to 'thunderous applause' from a critical and generally well-informed film-going elite. One of Berlin's famous Wertheim department stores joined in the film's promotion with great enthusiasm, hiring a handsome, articulate 17-year-old engineering student, Wernher von Braun, as compere.

Wernher Maximilian von Braun was born in March 1912 at Wirsitz in the German province of Posen, the son of Baron Magnus von Braun and Emmy von Quistrop. The young von Braun took readily to science and music and was soon excelling in mathematics and physics, subjects which would serve him well as he developed an interest in space travel. He became well versed in the teachings of Oberth, Nebel, Winkler, Valier and Ley, and was studying at the Berlin Institute of Technology, Charlottenburg, when he was invited to join the VfR. At Charlottenburg, he studied under Professor Doktor Karl Becker, an *oberstleutnant* (lieutenant colonel) in the Weapons Department of the *Reichswehr* (German National Defence), and devotee of innovative weapons, typically the huge First World War 'Paris Gun', before concentrating on liquid-fuelled rocket motors. It was Becker who would bring von Braun together with the highly talented engineer and artillery officer *Hauptmann* (Captain) Walter Dornberger in a partnership which would become central to the story of military rocket development in the Second World War and post-war exploration of space.

By 1929 Oberth and the rocket engineer Rudolf Nebel were also working on liquid propellants, now specifically for a series of small, low cost, *Minimum Rakete* (Mirak) rockets, powered by liquid oxygen and petrol. During their work tragedy struck with the death of Max Valier on 17 May 1930 when a mixture of kerosene, water and liquid oxygen exploded in a pressurised combustion chamber, this causing such public concern that Nebel's team decided to move the Mirak-1 trials away from prying eyes in Berlin to a farm at Bernstadt, Saxony.

By now it had become clear that a dedicated launch area was needed for testing the rapidly developing rocket technologies and the VfR seized the opportunity to take over a redundant ammunition depot at Reinickendorf in the northern Berlin suburb of Cité Pasteur, near Tegel Airport. This four-square-kilometre site, soon to be known as *Raketenflugplatz* (Rocket Airport) opened for business in September 1930 and it was there that the trials on the Mirak series of rockets continued.

The initial, static, tests of the Mirak-1 had been successful, but on its first launch the oxygen tank burst, destroying the rocket. The Mirak-2 fared better, a number of successful tests having been completed with a modified cooling system before it too suffered the same fate as its predecessor, the liquid oxygen cooling system being held to blame in both cases. By now, however, the rocketeers' work had attracted some wealthy backers and, undeterred by the early failures, the VfR continued its experiments with a new 'Repulsor' series, based on the Mirak but with the combustion chambers now cooled by water inside a double-walled aluminium skin. On its first launch, on 14 May 1931, Repulsor-1 reached a height of 200 feet, as did Repulsor-2, a week later, while Repulsor-3 climbed to 600 feet and Repulsor-4s continued the success story, ultimately achieving 5,000 feet over a range of 3,000 yards, before being recovered by parachute for further use.

While the VfR continued its work, other German rocket scientists and engineers were also having some success with their rockets, using both liquid and solid propellants. In March 1931 Reinholt Tiling and Karl Poggensee began launching their solid-fuel rockets, some carrying an altimeter, velocity indicator and cameras, up to heights of 6,000 feet, before they were recovered successfully by parachute. Tiling capitalised on this with his 'Post Office' rocket, which carried 188 postcards to a specified destination, and returned them, to argue the safety and speed of this innovative way of delivering the mail. He then took his rockets to Wangerooge, in the East Friesland Islands, where one reached a height of 30,000 feet, this attracting the attention of the *Reichsmarine*, which had been experimenting with rockets since 1929. Tragedy struck the rocket fraternity again when, on 10 October 1933, Tiling died of injuries sustained when one of his rockets exploded in his workshop. Meanwhile, Hugo Huckel and Johannes Winkler powered their small 'Huckel-Winkler 1' to a height of 1,000 feet, using a mix of liquid methane and liquid oxygen, from a site near Dessau, but their success was shortlived; in 1932 their 'Huckel-Winkler 2' rose to only 10 feet, before exploding on a range near Pillau, East Prussia. This was a dangerous time of 'trial and error'.

Just when rocket science was beginning to enjoy real progress, internal tensions in Germany, the great depression of 1931-32 and emergence of a new political order, began to intrude. The VfR, with its primary interest in space, was now dying a slow death, affected by the new conditions and the withdrawal of financial sponsors. Membership dropped to 300 in 1932 as more members found themselves unable to pay the subscription, while the *Reichswehr* (German Armed Forces), with scant interest in space, turned their attention to the military applications of rocketry. Seeing the writing on the wall, Nebel wrote a paper on the utility of rockets to supplement long-range artillery, quickly triggering a visit to the Rocket Airport by Lieutenant Colonel Becker and Captain Dornberger, from the German Weapons Department, to view the enhanced facilities there and discuss possible ways ahead for the rocket as a weapon. As a result Nebel received a small contract, with the necessary funding, conditional on the production of a rocket which could reach an altitude of 10,000 feet. To that end, work began at once, and the first of these rockets was launched in July 1932 at a new army proving ground, *Versuchsstelle West* (Experimental Station West), at Kummersdorf. The launch was a failure. The rocket rose a few hundred feet, before becoming unstable and careering off horizontally to crash a short distance away. As a result, Becker refused to pay the 1,367 Reichsmarks contracted, while cutting all ties with Nebel and the VfR – thus signalling the end of the amateur 'space club'.

While the Germans took the lead, other countries were dabbling in rocket science. In 1924 the Russians had set up the 'Central Bureau for the Study of the Problems of Rockets', and the 'All-Union Society for the Study of Inter-Planetary Flight'. Then, in 1932, the Russian space pioneer Fridrikh Tsander published a thesis 'Problems of Flight by Means of Reactive Devices' and this was followed, in 1935, by Glusko's 'Rockets, their Construction and Utilisation', while a powerful team of Russian scientists, sponsored by their government, tested a variety of liquid-fuelled rocket engines. From all this theoretical and practical work emerged two small rockets, the GIRD-X, which reached 1,300 feet in 1933, and the 'Aviavnito', which achieved 10,000 feet in 1936.

In 1928 the Austrian Dr Franz von Hoefft, of Vienna's *Gesellschaft für Hohenforschung* (Society for High Altitude Research), had begun to examine a number of options for rocket development. In 1931 he and his Austrian colleague Friedrich Schmiedl launched a solid-fuel rocket, to carry mail between Schockel, Radegund and Kumberg, inspiring fellow scientist Gerhard Zucker to attempt to do likewise in a cross-channel flight to Great Britain – but all their rockets exploded when launched. The Italians had also joined the party with Crocco and Riccardo Corelli carrying out tests in 1929 to show again that solid propellants were not suitable for long-range rockets and leading to an examination of such alternative liquid combinations as petrol/nitrogen dioxide, trinitroglycerine/methyl alcohol and trinitroglycerine/nitromethane. These trials were abandoned in 1935, due to lack of funding.

The American Interplanetary Society (AIS) was also developing rockets, fuelled by a mixture of liquid oxygen and petrol, and was soon learning its own lessons the hard way. The AIS-1 was said to have been 'a model of thrift and ingenuity', with an aluminium water jacket fashioned from a cocktail shaker, wooden fins and a parachute holder made from an aluminium saucepan. Static tests took place in 1932, during which 60 pounds of thrust (measured on rudimentary spring scales) was generated for 20 to 30 seconds. The rocket was launched at Great Kills, New York, on 14 May 1933, only for the oxygen tank to burst at 250 feet. A second model, which took to the air on 9 September 1934, reached an unsatisfactory 1,338 feet, after which the tests were abandoned. Thereafter, the AIS was committed to the support of a variety of other national rocket projects, using both solid and liquid fuels, but none enjoyed any great success before all the trials were suspended in 1939, at the outbreak of the Second World War. Suffice it to say that, in the 1930s, no other nation could match the achievements of the German rocket scientists.

The lure of space had motivated many of the big names in German rocket research, giving impetus to rocket development, albeit with some purists at the helm being less enthusiastic about the military applications. Although it could not have escaped notice, many also seemed to pay little heed to the rise of the Nazi party, some even showing a dangerous contempt for Hitler and his cohorts, with all that this might mean for their future. But it was the resurgence of German military aspirations which kept the rocketeers in business, as the Nazi hierarchy in the 1930s attempted to navigate its way around the constraints imposed on them by the Treaty of Versailles. Looking for alternative military concepts and technologies, they perceived that the rocket was one way to go. The more foresighted pragmatists in the rocket community played down any devotion to space and accepted that tacit allegiance to the whims and wills of those then wielding power might be the best, indeed possibly the only, way to achieve their ultimate objectives. Thus began a new chapter in the evolution of the rocket in Germany against the background of a revitalised nation, devoted to innovation, industry and a determination to find a new place in history.

However, it was clear that a hard core of Germany's rocket men remained obsessed by the 'lure of space', loudly applauding Walter Dornberger at a celebration in Peenemünde to mark the first fully successful launch and flight of their A4 embryo missile, when he said:

> This is the first time we have invaded space with our rocket. Mark this well, we have used space as a bridge between two points on the earth; we have proven rocket propulsion practicable for space travel. This third day of October 1942 is the first of a new era of transportation – that of space travel.

In the meantime, however, there was a war to be won.

Chapter 2

Deadly Innovation

Although the German Army (*Heer*) Weapons Agency, given the name *Heeres Waffenamt (HWA)* in 1922, already incorporated a research and development department, the *Heereswaffenamt Prüfwesen (Wa Prüf)*, the serious work on German military rockets did not begin until 1931, when Captain Walter Dornberger took the lead with a team of aspiring rocketeers, including Rudolf Nebel, Klaus Riedel, Heinrich Grünow and the rising star Wernher von Braun. Making good use of the fundamentals prescribed by Hermann Oberth, they were to kick-start the nation's rocket development in its new direction – that of military application, under the ever watchful eyes of the *Wehrmacht* (German Armed Forces). This was grist to the mill for Dornberger, a gunnery officer who recognised the limitations of artillery, with even the mighty, but hardly mobile 'Paris Gun', limited to some eighty miles in range, with a relatively small projective, a low rate of fire and poor accuracy. He saw the rocket more as a supplement or alternative to long-range artillery than as a replacement for the manned bomber aircraft and believed that, initially, he could double the maximum range achieved by contemporary artillery with a rocket carrying a one-ton warhead. Ultimately he hoped to build a successor weighing 100 tons, with a 10-ton warhead over ever greater ranges –and the *Aggregate* (Aggregate) series of rockets was a first step in that direction.

Dornberger's new group was based first at the old military range at Kummersdorf, south of Berlin, and it was there that its first rocket, the Aggregate 1 (A1), was tested on 21 December 1932. The A1, 4 feet 7 inches long and 1 foot in diameter, had a take-off weight of 330lb; it was fuelled by a mixture of alcohol and liquid oxygen, to generate 300 pounds of thrust for 16 seconds. This first attempt was a failure, with the A1 blowing up on the launch pad, and because it was suspected that the heavy gyroscope installed in the nose would also render it unstable in flight, the A1 was abandoned in favour of the A2. This was a larger rocket, 5 feet 3 inches long and weighing 236lb, powered by a new engine producing 3,000 pounds of thrust for

50 seconds. This time the stabilisation gyroscopes were positioned in the centre of the rocket's body, between the oxygen and alcohol fuel tanks. Two A2s, named *Max* and *Mintz* (after the cartoon characters of that time) were launched on 19 and 20 December 1934 respectively, from a Baltic site at Borkum, where a large group of military and civilian VIPs, watched them climb to heights above 10,000 feet.

In a historic milestone which would have worldwide consequences, Hitler unilaterally repudiated the Treaty of Versailles in 1935, freeing Germany from all the military constraints it had imposed. This released unprecedented funds for a massive rearmament programme and gave rocket development new impetus. Within the reorganisation of the German Ordnance Department, the rocket group was designated *Wa Prüf 11* (Weapons Testing Branch 11). Dornberger guarded this branch jealously, but he needed all the help he could get to further his cause, so he welcomed the interest shown by Lieutenant Colonel Wolfram von Richthofen, head of the Air Ministry Technical Office and cousin of that legendary First World War pilot, the 'Red Baron', in the use of rockets to power a fighter fast enough to compete with the Allied aircraft then in the pipeline. To that end, von Richthofen visited Kummersdorf first in January 1935 and joined members of *Wa Prüf 11*, the Air Ministry and the aircraft designer, Willy Messerschmitt, when they visited the independent German engineer Paul

Schmitt, who was developing a pulse-jet engine for both missiles and aircraft. In this Schmitt failed but valuable lessons were learned from his research, which would help the Argus engine company to perfect a pulse-jet engine for the flying bomb which would be nurtured later by the *Luftwaffe* (German Air Force).

By 1936 the facilities at Kummersdorf had been greatly improved, with two new static test stands, mobile test rigs and the extensive support facilities necessary to accommodate the much larger A3. The A3 measured 22 feet long and 2 feet 4 inches in diameter and weighed 1,650lb at lift-off; its engine provided 3,300 pounds of thrust for 45 seconds, using a pressure-fed propellant of liquid oxygen and ethanol, and it carried

Dr Walter Dornberger.
(Author, Courtesy HTM Peenemünde)

The First World War 'Paris Gun' set standards for the Second World War. (Author, Courtesy HTM Peenemünde)

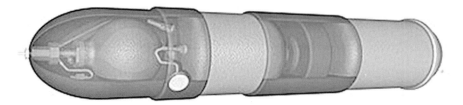

Aggregate A2, the beginnings of a military rocket. (Author, Courtesy HTM Peenemünde)

an inertial guidance system. The problem of how to stabilise the rocket without the rotation imparted to a shell in the rifled barrel of a gun was solved by incorporating a simple but reliable gyroscope-based 'autopilot', designed by Dr Karl Fieber and produced by Kreiselgeräte GmbH (Gyro Devices Ltd). The A3 had narrow fins, to give aerodynamic stability at supersonic speeds, telemetry to measure temperatures and pressures in flight and a radio receiver, using on-board power, to take commands from the ground to shut the engine down in the air. German rocket development was gathering pace.

Despite the improvements at Kummersdorf, it soon became clear that the weapons range there was too small to accommodate new technologies or serve all potential users, and too open to public scrutiny, so the search began for a more suitable alternative. The Baltic island of Rügen came to mind, but this had been commandeered by the all-powerful German Labour Front as a 'strength through joy' recreational area, an initiative known to be greatly favoured by Adolf Hitler – and so inviolate. It was Werner von Braun who found an ideal site, on the Baltic Island of Usedom where his father used to go duck hunting, specifically the Peenemünde peninsula to the north of the island, and it was there that the HWA established one of its most important weapons proving grounds: *Heeresversuchsanstalt Peenemünde (HVP)*

Usedom, sixty miles long and twenty-eight wide, was indeed a very suitable location for rocket research and development. The peninsula consisted largely of flat, sandy soil, much of which was covered by pine forests; it had a scattering of settlements, with Peenemünde village in the north-west offering a small port. Monitoring equipment, sited along a 250-mile stretch of the Baltic/Pomeranian coastline to the east, would allow rocket flights to be tracked after launch from Peenemünde, while restricted access to the island gave a high measure of security. Moreover, the tiny island of Greifswalder Oie, north-north-east of Peenemünde, could be an invaluable adjunct to the main range on Usedom.

So it was that, on 2 April 1936, the German Air Ministry paid the local town of Wolgast 750,000 Reichsmarks for the whole of the northern peninsula, the cost shared between the German army and air force. The village of Peenemünde was evacuated and work began on the infrastructure, the air force taking the lead in the construction, unfettered by the army's traditional ways and conventional wisdoms. This resulted in state-of-the-art research, development, test and production installations, unrivalled anywhere in the world, with the army and air force occupying two distinct sectors.

The Army Research Centre was located *at* Peenemünde Ost (Peenemünde East), sub-divided into *Werk Ost* (Eastern Works) and *Werk Süd* (Southern Works*)*. To the north-east, where the forest gave way to a sandy shoreline, nine rocket test stands were built, the largest and most prominent being Test Stand VII, from which most of the surface-to-surface rockets would be launched, while three more stands, for rocket engine tests, were sited north-west of Karlshagen. Farther north on the peninsula, at *Werk West* (Western Works*)*, lay the Air Force Test Site, with its rudimentary airfield, test stands and flying-bomb launch pads.

Peenemünde Power Station, looking north, largely unscathed by Allied bombing, survives to this day. (Author, Courtesy HTM Peenemünde)

Peenemünde's Liquid Oxygen Plant – still standing in 2013. (Author, Courtesy HTM Peenemünde)

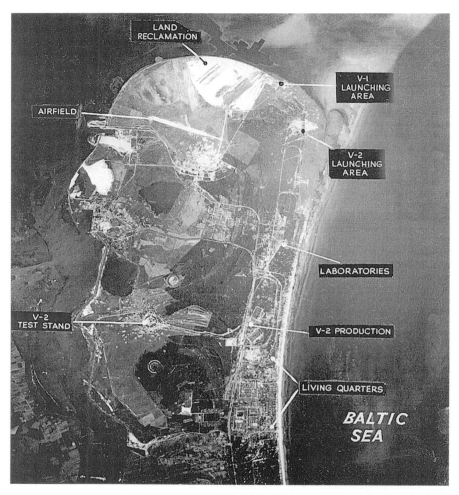

The Peenemünde Peninsula. (Author's Collection, Courtesy HTM Peenemünde)

Between the army and air force sections, a huge, 30,000-KW, coal-fired power station and a liquid oxygen factory, fundamental to the new technologies, each served the whole complex, while an electric railway linked all its main components. To the south, a well-landscaped housing estate was built to accommodate the 'privileged' workers, said to number well in excess of 1,200. Beyond that, at Karlshagen, lay Community Barracks East, originally intended for the German military but made into a *FZ-Arbeitslager* (labour camp), for some 1,500 male prisoners employed by the air force, while a concentration camp cut from the forest farther south, at Trassenheide, kept thousands of slave labourers in appalling conditions. This was big business.

The first 350 rocket scientists and technicians began to move from Kummersdorf to Peenemünde in April 1937, although the facilities there were far from complete; indeed, the establishment did not reach full strength until 1940. Until then, the all-important engine development team, under Dr Walter Thiel, continued its work at Kummersdorf. Dr Thiel was born in 1910 and soon proved to be an outstanding scholar, excelling at all levels in his chosen subject, chemistry, *summa cum laude,* to gain his doctorate in 1934. The German Army Weapons Office was quick to spot his talents and Dornberger, then a major at Kummersdorf, recruited him into the Aggregate team. Ultimately it was Thiel who would be responsible for perfecting the engine which would take the much vaunted A4 (V2) rocket to London; he would not, however, live to see the dreadful results of his work.

In April 1937 Dornberger persuaded Rudolf Hermann, Hermann Kurzweg and Walter Haeussermann, the best aerodynamicists then available, to join his team, ready to make full use of the world's most sophisticated, supersonic wind tunnel, then being built at Peenemünde. When complete, expected to be in late 1942, this would enable tests to be carried out at speeds of up to Mach 4.4 (4.4 times the speed of sound), importantly with an innovative desiccant system (moisture remover) to reduce the condensation misting caused by the use of liquid oxygen. Pending completion of the Peenemünde tunnel, Rudolf Hermann carried out initial tests on the A3's design, in a small wind tunnel at Aachen Technical University. These tests suggested that the rocket could deviate from its intended flightpath in crosswinds, that the fins might burn up as the exhaust expanded in the lower air densities at height, and that, in any event, these fins were too small to control the rocket at high altitudes. Hermann Kurzweg thought likewise, having towed models of the A3 behind his car at 100km/h. Time would tell but, following satisfactory static tests at Kummersdorf, the A3 was ready for flight trials at the end of 1937.

With the necessary launch and test facilities yet to be completed at Peenemünde, the first four A3s were launched from Greifswalder Oie, where concrete launch pads and bunkers had been built for the purpose. On 4 December 1937, in appalling weather conditions, the first A3 lifted off successfully, but after a few seconds its recovery parachute deployed prematurely before burning off in the rocket's plume, sending the rocket spinning into wind and crashing a short distance from the launch pad. This happened again to the second A3 a few days later, after which the parachutes were disabled for the remaining two firings – but again the rockets spun into wind and crashed. Exhaustive examinations concluded that the predictions from the early wind tunnel tests had been correct, that the rocket did indeed veer off the intended track in crosswinds, beyond the capability of the Kreiselgeräte guidance and control system to correct. As a result of these failures, work on the A3 was abandoned and the Aggregate team gave its full attention to the A4 and A5.

With Wernher von Braun as technical director, Walter Thiel as his deputy and engine expert, and Dornberger responsible for research, the rocket programmes at Peenemünde now developed apace in the technical design, guidance, aeroballistics, test, wind tunnel and manufacturing departments. Dornberger's ambitions knew few bounds, beginning with the establishment of *Gruppe IV* (Group IV), within *Wa Pruf 11,* to plan and construct the facilities required then and in the future, with a little added everywhere as contingencies against unforeseen circumstances – and indeed dramatic events were now unfolding elsewhere in a turbulent Germany, which might threaten progress at the HVP.

Germany in the 1930s was never without its political intrigue, as the Nazi party overthrew the Weimar parliamentary democracy, increased its power generally and dominated the military, defying traditions, and ousting those in its hierarchy who did not display absolute and unequivocal loyalty to the Führer, Adolf Hitler. All Jews were removed from authoritative positions, the trades unions were disbanded and a new organisation, the *Deutsche Arbeitsfront (DAF),* the German Labour Front, began to flex its muscles. The majority of the new leaders were neither politicians nor businessmen, industrialists, scientists, engineers or technocrats, many being pseudo-intellectuals, such as Himmler, anti-intellectuals like Martin Bormann, and they were supported by an army of self-serving *gauleiters* (petty officials). From 1933 government economic 'centralisation' became the name of the game, largely to the detriment of commercial interests and fast-developing technologies, but military expansion, as a whole, was given a high priority.

Transition to the new order was far from smooth, with allegations of human frailties often used to weed out those seen to be disloyal or simply weak links, one such victim being General Werner von Fritsch, *Oberkommando des Heeres (OKH),* C-in-C of the Army, who had given his full support to the work at Kummersdorf in 1936, and the concept of a more extensive rocket development site at Peenemünde. He was forced to resign in February 1938, on suspicions of homosexuality, to be replaced as head of the OKH, by *Generalfeldmarschall (*Field Marshal) Walther von Brauchitsch. Hitler disbanded the War Ministry and created the *Oberkommando der Wehrmacht* (OKW), the Armed Forces High Command, to be headed by Field Marshal Wilhelm Keitel, and it was he who would preside over massive growth in military assets, at a critical point in the development of the rocket for war. Having followed the rocketeers' early progress, Fritsch and Brauchitsch had visited Kummersdorf in 1936 where they had pledged their support and the necessary funds. As artillery officers they were attracted to new weapons which could outrange contemporary guns, might deliver a greater punch, be more mobile and provide an alternative to the Luftwaffe's bombers, over which they had no direct control.

One of the first actions taken by von Brauchitsch was to order the planning and construction of an A4 production plant at Peenemünde, to be controlled by a subsection of *Wa Prüf 11*, set up by Dornberger in January 1939, with Herr G. Schubert, a senior army civil servant, at the helm. Notwithstanding this decision, *Fertigungshalle-1 'F-1'* (Mass Production Plant No.1) would not be completed until mid-1943, mainly because of Hitler's continued indecision over the priority and funding to be accorded to the work being carried out at Peenemünde.

Dornberger was all too aware that the future of the A4, intended to become the rocket with which Germany could bombard London, needed the full support of the Nazi Party and Hitler himself. Accordingly, on 23 March 1939, he invited the Führer, his deputy, Rudolf Hess, Chief of Staff Martin Bormann, von Brauchitsch and Army Ordnance Chief General Karl Becker, to a progress meeting at Kummersdorf. He had prepared himself well, to capitalise on Hitler's enthusiasm for innovative new weapons with which to prosecute his wars, as he described the research in hand, progress achieved with the A3 (referring to cutaway models of the missile), future concepts

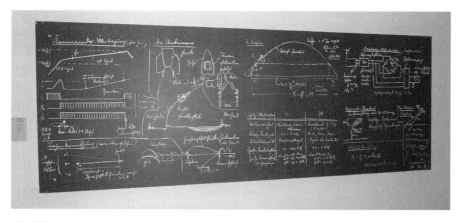

Blackboard 'jottings' by Wernher von Braun, believed to have been rescued from Peenemünde. (Author, Courtesy la Coupole)

and technologies, stressing the potential for expediting rocket development, before the group toured the facilities and witnessed engine tests. He assured the Führer that the A4 would be constructed largely of steel, rather than the aluminium so urgently needed for aircraft and that the missile could, given the right priority, be operational by 1942. He was, however, surprised and disappointed by Hitler's lack of penetrating questions and indeed his apparent disinterest in the rocket's likely contribution as a weapon of war, concluding that there was more work to be done to convince him.

Despite some sections still not fully operational, the Peenemünde facility was declared operational at the end of 1939, with Colonel Leo Zanssen in command. Having invaded Poland in September, Germany was now at war with France and Britain, and had fully mobilised its manpower. The armed forces and every section of industry were now demanding priority in their share of the men and materials available, but there was no clear system for allocating priorities in an already failing four-year economic plan, and this did not bode well for the rocket men. However, Dornberger, knowing that he had the support of von Brauchitsch, hoped that he would press for the HVP to be given enough resources for the missile assembly facility, and for rocket development to be 'pushed forward by all possible means', as being 'particularly urgent for national defence'. Be that as it may, Hitler, Keitel and Hermann Göring, the Commander-in-Chief of the Luftwaffe, chose to give priority to those activities of immediate importance to the war. There was, however, some encouragement in May 1941, when Hitler changed his mind again, giving the rocketeers more – but still not enough to achieve the then delivery target of eighteen A4s by September 1941. The long term effects of this indecisive, stop/go programme would turn out to be very significant in the final stages of the war.

Before the A4 missile materialised, the A5 rocket, a diminutive version measuring 20 feet long and 3 feet in diameter, was introduced as a test vehicle. Aerodynamically identical to the A4, the A5 incorporated many of its components; it included an inertial guidance control designed by Siemens, a radio-command system to enable the engine to cut off from the ground and a recovery by parachute to be initiated, and an engine which ran on a similar alcohol/liquid oxygen mix. Multiple wind-tunnel tests had resulted in small, streamlined tail surfaces. The rocket was designed to manoeuvre into a ballistic attitude when the gyroscopes tilted in the desired direction of flight, causing the autopilot to send signals to the servos attached to the exhaust vanes, which would then deflect the blast to tilt the rocket over, while correcting any drift caused by crosswinds. The all-important gyros

Rheinbote. Long-range rocket gun. (Author Courtesy HTM Peenemünde)

were designed to control the tilt during the curved flight path and apply course corrections as required. Pending delivery of the final gyro-autopilot system, the firm of Siemens installed an interim control fit. The A5 trials would provide data on ballistic shape, transonic behaviour, and guidance throughout the burning portion of the rocket's flight.

At this stage the aim was to produce ten A5s a month and the first airborne 'drop test' models were delivered to Peenemünde in spring 1938, but it would be more than a year before they were cleared for airborne release. In September 1939 a Heinkel He-111 dropped an A5 from 20,000 feet, to achieve supersonic speeds at 3,000 feet, the stabilising fins keeping the dummy missiles within 5 degrees of the vertical, before the retarding parachute slowed the descent for them to 'splash down' safely – for post-flight examination. Ground launches followed at Greifswalder Oie, the first two without the stabilising system or recovery parachutes, merely to test the pre-set trajectories. The next two climbed vertically until their motors shut down at 45 seconds and momentum carried them above 30,000 feet before a signal from the ground deployed their

Attempts to increase the range of the A4 rocket, by attaching 'wings' to create the A4b, failed, and trials were abandoned after one unsuccessful launch. (Author, Courtesy HTM Peenemünde)

parachutes, for them to splash down and be recovered, close to Oie. In the next test, the all-important guidance system performed faultlessly, to great applause from the ground. This A5 was seen to follow the programmed trajectory, tilt perfectly on time, then take up an easterly heading and level out as required, before the parachute brought the rocket down safely. The Siemens' system continued to come up to expectations in the many more tests which followed, reaching heights in excess of 40,000 feet and ranges of eleven miles, the results confirming the theoretical calculations and predictions for the A4, thus vindicating the use of the A5 as a test vehicle for the ultimate weapon. Dornberger was euphoric, allegedly heard to say, 'Now I can see our goal clearly, and the way that leads to it', predicting that production of the A4 could be underway by 1943 – but that would prove to be a little too optimistic.

"Meanwhile, the Luftwaffe was beginning to show interest in work being conducted by civilian firms on a flying bomb, and by the end of the 1930s their collective efforts were being co-ordinated at Peenemünde West. The idea for a pulse-jet engine had been explored first by the Russian Victor Karavodine in 1906, then by the Frenchman George Marconnet in 1910. However, it was Paul Schmidt's 'Schmidt Duct' engine which, in 1933, caught the attention of the German Air Ministry and, by the end of the decade, Fritz Gosslau of the Argus Engine Company, and Robert Lusser of the Fieseler Aircraft Company, were ready to offer their design for a relatively simple flying bomb.

The concept was based on a small, pilotless aircraft, driven by a cheap but powerful version of the Argus As-014, pulse-jet engine, in which airflow forced through shutters at the mouth of a tube into a combustion chamber would be mixed with a standard petrol fuel spray and ignited. This would

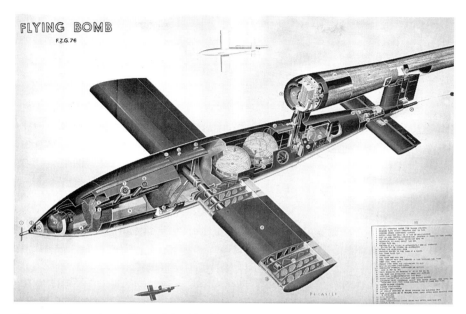

FLYING BOMB
F.Z.G.76

Above: Schematic outline of the Fi 103 (V1) flying bomb. (Author's Collection)

cause an explosion which closed the front shutters, forcing the expanding air out through the jet pipe at the rear to provide the thrust. As soon as the pressure in the tube dropped, the shutters would open again, and this cycle repeated many times a minute, emitting a pulsating rhythm. The airframe would have a wingspan of about seventeen feet, on a fuselage some twenty-five-feet long, with the pulse-jet mounted above a conventional tail assembly. With the strong airflow needed for the engine to operate effectively, a powerful steam-driven catapult was needed to drive the little aircraft up an inclined ramp, aligned with its target, giving it enough flying speed for the pulse-jet to take over. When sufficient data had been collected to confirm a viable concept, Argus and Fieseler went to the German Air Ministry with firm proposals on 28 April 1942. Their confidence would be well rewarded.

For those at Peenemünde, it was now vital that their twin projects, the rocket and the flying bomb, be seen to be moving inexorably towards operational status and this, in a politically charged Germany, bred strange bedfellows. Typically, *Reichsführer-SS* Himmler, the head of the much feared *Schutzstaffel* (SS), in seeking to extend his influence, began to take an interest in developments at the HVP in 1940, awarding Wernher von Braun the honorary rank of *untersturmführer* (lieutenant) in the SS, this simple action attracting the attention and positive interest among other Germany leaders and industrialists.

While Aggregate rockets and the flying bomb were stealing the limelight, other German weapon interests were looking into the use of associated technologies. Rheinmetall-Borsig AG (RMB) had been invited to submit ideas for a rocket-assisted take-off (RATO) unit to expedite the take-off of large cargo aircraft now being produced, while German anti-aircraft gunners were looking into the practicability of using rockets for air defence, possibly adapting the *Wasserfall* variant of the A4 to that end. Meanwhile, field gunners, on the lookout for long-range, lightweight and fully mobile supplements to their heavy artillery, were evaluating a relatively simple, long-range, four-stage, solid-fuelled rocket, christened *Rheinbote*. More ambitious was the *Hochdruckpumpe* (High Pressure Pump), a massive, static, multi-barrel cannon, primarily for the bombardment of London from sites in the Pas de Calais. All these ventures are outlined in Chapter Nine

For Germany the 1930s were years of extraordinary technological innovation, which brought great advances in rocket science for military applications and the use of space. By their dogged persistence, Dornberger, von Braun, Thiel and others laid the foundations for the new weapons of war, but now they faced rigorous test programmes before they could be deployed operationally.

Chapter 3

Testing Times

Having learned much throughout the exhaustive, frustrating but latterly rewarding work on the A3 and A5, the rocketeers at the HVP now concentrated all their efforts on the A4, which had started life in 1938, and would become their ultimate objective in the Second World War – as the V2. The requirement was for a rocket which could carry a large warhead over the greatest practicable range and Dornberger was uncompromising in his demands calling for accuracy, typically calling for no more than 2- to 3-metre error for every 1,000 metres in range, with a missile which would be transportable on existing roads and railways in continental Europe.

To satisfy these requirements, the A4 (V2) would measure 46 feet long and 5 feet in diameter, weigh 13.6 tons with 9 tons of fuel aboard, and carry a warhead of one ton consisting of a relatively stable amatol explosive, fired by two electrical, instantaneous contact fuses designed to maximise blast, all encased in a fibreglass jacket to maintain the required temperature. Behind the warhead, the control compartment contained the gyros and radio equipment and in the centre of the rocket were two separate tanks for the alcohol and liquid-oxygen fuel. Then came the fuel pumps, hydrogen peroxide and permanganate tanks, the combustion chamber and venturi. At the tail end of the rocket, the four fins were fitted with the external rudders, acting with four internal, graphite vanes (jet rudders), which operated in the rocket's exhaust, their electro-hydraulic servo motors, cooling systems and associated piping. An LEV-3 guidance system consisted of two free gyros, one for yaw and roll, the other for pitch and tilt, while a Kreiselgeräte PIGA gyro-type accelerometer and a simple analogue computer were incorporated to pre-set propulsion cut-off. An alternative system was based on a 3-gyro, 3-axis stabilised platform. In the field the missile would be aligned precisely with its target from a pre-surveyed location. Some later versions of the rocket were kept on the required track by radio beams. At its best, the A4's engine, fuelled by a mixture of 74 per cent ethanol/water (B-Stoff) and liquid oxygen (A-Stoff), delivered the required 55,000–66,000lbs of thrust for 65 seconds, a turbo-pump driven by steam generated from the catalytic decomposition of hydrogen peroxide, boosting the flow of alcohol and oxygen into the combustion chamber. Much attention was paid to the all-important heating and cooling of critical areas in the missile. The engine was tested successfully in March 1940, but much more had to be done before the A4 took to the skies.

Nineteen-forty was a year of mixed fortunes for the A4 team. First, it lost a firm supporter in Karl Becker, head of the Army Ordnance Office, who committed suicide in May. Then, paradoxically, it suffered when Germany defeated France so quickly that the Nazi leaders no longer thought it necessary to expedite the rocket programme, and the resources available to it, the problem exacerbated by the withdrawal of the foreign workers at the HVP, to enhance security at the site. Then came the good news that Becker was to be replaced by General Emil Leeb, another rocket devotee, that von Brauchitsch had convinced the Armament Ministry that the HVP needed more resources, and that the formidable Albert Speer, another invaluable ally, would take charge of construction at the HVP, *inter alia* resurrecting work on its production unit. Moreover, the German defeat in the Battle of Britain counteracted the effects of its rapid victory over France and gave more impetus to the rocket programme. However, in June 1941, the German invasion of Russia placed further demands on manpower and materials, and the Minister of Armaments, Dr Fritz Todt, reduced the HVP's funding once more.

Given these fluctuations in fortune, Dornberger felt compelled to remind the German hierarchy that the rocket and the flying bomb were both adjuncts and alternatives to long-range artillery and to the manned bomber aircraft, and reiterated their attractions. Again, in August 1941, he updated Hitler, Keitel and General Fromm, commander of the Reserve Army, on progress at Peenemünde and persuaded the Führer to allocate more resources to the HVP. Despite this, Fritz Todt continued to keep a tight rein on the funds needed by the HVP, allegedly using this as a bargaining chip in his attempts to take control of the *Herresweffenamt* (Army Weapons Office), a move strongly opposed in the *Wehrmacht*. All this in-fighting and turbulence had a detrimental effect on the morale of the rocketeers, some of whom turned their thoughts once more to rockets for space exploration, their first love, rather than their use in warfare. Sensing this drift from the official mandate, Dornberger pressed his staff for completion of working drawings necessary to determine what was needed to produce an initial batch of 600 military A4s.

TESTING TIMES

On 8 February 1942 Fritz Todt was killed in an air crash and was replaced as the Armaments Minister by the more popular Albert Speer. However, this was quickly followed by another major cut in funding and a reduction in the allocation of the all-important hydrogen peroxide. The project was then put at further risk when the first complete A4 exploded during a static test. Fearing another loss of momentum, Dornberger urged the OKW to accept that, with a projected output of 5,000 rockets per year, Germany could keep up a bombardment of lucrative targets in England without warning, night and day, in every weather, immune from air defences, adversely affecting British morale while reducing pressure on the Luftwaffe. These were persuasive and timely arguments, particularly in the wake of the RAF's devastating attacks on Lübeck (March 1942) and Cologne (May 1942). Hitler now saw the rocket as the only viable means of exacting revenge in kind, but he demanded that Dornberger's offer be multiplied by a factor of ten – a production rate of 50,000 rockets per year. This wholly unrealistic figure was quickly and dramatically reduced, but all the necessary prerequisites to operate the rocket in the field (procedures, training, equipment *et al*) were initiated at once, in the hands of *Versuchskommando Nord* (Experimental Unit North), perhaps in the hope of giving the impression of more rapid progress.

Generalmajor Dr Walter Dornberger at Peenemünde. (Author, Courtesy Peenemünde)

On 3 October 1942, after three failures, the fourth A4 launched successfully from Test Stand VII at Peenemünde; it followed the pre-set trajectory, albeit a little steeply, to a height of 50 miles, achieving a speed of 3,300 mph and landing, as planned, 120 miles down the range. This was the first of the A4s to reach outer space and the team was ecstatic. Moreover, the fact that things were now going badly for the Germans on the Russian front and in North Africa worked in their favour, Speer arguing that it was now even more important that the A4 be rushed into service as soon as possible, and Hitler acquiesced. In December 1942 he ordered the rocket into mass production and six months later gave the project the highest priority in materials and manpower, while finally agreeing to the construction of a production facility at the HVP and calling for the immediate construction of impregnable concrete launch sites in the Pas de Calais – within range of London.

This prompted renewed competition for control of the new weapons, with *Reichsführer-SS* Heinrich Himmler, head of the Gestapo and SS, paying an early visit to Peenemünde to make a case for the whole project to be placed under the control of the SS. The Führer demurred, and did so again when Himmler tried a second time in January 1943 – but that would not be the end of the matter. Seeing the writing on the wall, Speer immediately consolidated his position by setting up 'development commissions' manned by all the best weapons designers and military minds available to review the best way ahead for the A4, while appointing the ruthless and dedicated Nazi General Gerd Degenkolb to oversee a special A4 committee as his 'hatchet man'. Degenkolb was ill-equipped for the role, having no knowledge or understanding of rocket technology, and his relationship with Dornberger suffered accordingly. Then, in early 1943, came another intrusion when Hitler ordered a *Entwicklungs-commission für Fernschiessen* (Development Commission for Long-Range Bombardment), under the elderly industrialist Dr Waldemar Petersen, to organise and control every aspect of the rocket and flying bomb organisations, and ultimately recommend which of the two missile projects, the rocket or the flying bomb – or both – should proceed. To those who had toiled away on the two missiles for years this was an unnecessary 'clumsy, unwieldy conglomerate', which did nothing to help either camp. To make matters worse, there were now allegations, true or false, of 'mismanagement and impropriety' in the HVP, with the incumbents accused of not operating 'in accordance with best business practices', where specialists and technicians were not employed efficiently. Dornberger, Heinz Mackels, Degenkolb's assistant, and Karl Hettlage,

Right and below:
The powerful
V2 rocket engine.
(Author, Courtesy
HTM Peenemünde)

the Munitions Minister's 'troubleshooter', were then ordered to consider the privatisation of the HVP, and Dornberger again needed all his skills to minimise these effects, and ward off another attempt by Himmler's SS, to take control of the missile installations.

By February 1943 arrangements were in hand to bring the A4s 20,000 components together for production at four locations: Peenemünde, the old airship works at Friedrichshafen, the Volkswagen factory at Fallersleben (Kassel) and the locomotive factory in Wiener-Neustadt (Austria). With insufficient, skilled labour now available in Germany, Fritz Sauckel, head of labour allocation, was authorised to recruit specially selected workers from other nations.

Behind the scenes, Armaments Minister Albert Speer, recognizing the potential value of both rocket and flying bomb, was bent on removing or at least reducing the increasingly unhelpful rivalry between the two project teams. On 26 May he hosted the Führer and a dazzling array of interested parties to a practical demonstration of both missiles, at Peenemünde – hoping that both would be at their best. It was not to be; while the two A4 performed well, the second flying 165 statute miles down the range for a pre-planned splash-down, neither of the two flying bombs impressed, the first crashing soon after launch and the second refusing to leave the ground. If this had been a decisive 'fly-off', the A4 would have won the day and the flying bomb would have been cancelled. However, Speer persisted, reiterating the arguments for and against each weapon, his conviction and persuasive power finally paying off when the bombardment committee recommended that the two missiles should continue to be developed in parallel, albeit with priority accorded to the rocket, and he issued an order to that effect on 2 June 1943.

On 7 July 1943 Hitler visited Peenemünde again where Dornberger and von Braun briefed the Führer on their success with the 'war winning' A4, and tempting him further with their predictions for a 100-ton, A10 giant, a rocket which could take a worthwhile warhead across the Atlantic to America – then already in the planning stage. With renewed enthusiasm, Hitler is said to have apologized for his early vacillation on the rocket; he promptly elevated Dornberger to the rank of *Generalmajor*, and on Speer's recommendation, von Braun to 'Professor' – just reward indeed for their extraordinary persistence. He then demanded that work on the huge, reinforced concrete launch sites for the A4, in the Pas de Calais, should continue, despite Dornberger's strong preference for multiple, highly mobile sites.

While there was still much work to do, and trials to be carried out on the A4 before it could be used in the war, training and deployment plans were already well advanced. *Lehr und Versuchs Batterie 444* (Training and Experimental Battery 444) was activated at Peenemünde in July 1943 to evaluate the weapon before deployment, develop firing procedures in the field and begin the training of launch and support crews. Three more batteries would follow, one destined for the huge concrete bunkers being prepared in France and two which would operate from tactical sites.

Back at Peenemünde all was not well. Dr Walter Thiel, and many of his V2 engine team, were exhausted by excessive workloads, with the impending transition from research to production and the relentless pressure on them to succeed. Thiel took himself off to a health farm

Four A4 (V2) test vehicles awaiting trials. (Author, Courtesy HTM Peenemünde)

and from there wrote of his concerns to von Braun, claiming that the V2 was still more of a complicated research vehicle than an operational missile and, on 17 August, offered his resignation – which von Braun promptly rejected. That night Thiel and all his family were killed during the massive raid on Peenemünde by the RAF.

In the early summer of 1943, following careful scrutiny of air reconnaissance photographs, evaluation of all other sources of intelligence, such as coded messages from courageous agents working on the site, and much debate at the highest levels it was decided that Peenemünde must be targeted by RAF Bomber Command with a maximum effort at the earliest opportunity (Chapter Eight). The raid, given the name Operation HYDRA was carried out on 17/18 August 1944 but was far from the success that was claimed. True, twenty-five buildings were destroyed within the experimental works, including the drawing office and the V2 assembly shop, together with many documents and records, and of course Dr Theil was among the 600 who died, most of them foreign workers, but including many good informants. However, most of the German rocket specialists had survived and their heroic actions had saved volumes of vital documents. Interestingly, neither the massive, very visible coal-fired power station, nor the Luftwaffe airfield, the flying bomb nor Me163 rocket-fighter development facilities at Peenemünde West, were on the target list – and they remain unscathed to this day.

Dornberger believed that HYDRA set the rocket schedule back two months, but these were crucial months, and it was clear that, if further interruptions to the programme were to be avoided, another V2 test facility would have to be found beyond the range of Allied bombers. The site chosen was at Blizna, deep into Poland. Also, it had already been accepted that the decentralized production and assembly sites for the two missiles at Peenemünde, Friedrichshafen, Fallerslaben and Wiener-Neustadt were no longer tenable, although they would continue to produce missiles until production was centralized, deep underground in an old gypsum mine in the Kohnstein (Harz) mountains, at Niedersachswerfen, north-west of Nordhausen.

To Dornberger's dismay, Speer charged Gerd Degenkolb, a man with no knowledge of rocket science, with overseeing the conversion of the twelve miles of caves, recently used to store fuel and oil reserves, into a massive industrial complex, not only for the production of both missiles, but also for that of the Luftwaffe's revolutionary Me262 jet fighter and Ar234 jet bomber. Himmler offered to provide the huge slave labour force needed to transform the caves, and to carry out mundane tasks thereafter, from the concentration camps, that at Buchenwald being a mere few miles to the east. *Brigadeführer* SS Hans Kammler, the engineer who had been involved in designing the notorious Nazi death camps, was given the job of mustering the force, and the first 100 inmates from Buchenwald arrived at Nordhausen on 27 August. The production company, Mittelwerk GmbH (Central Works Ltd), was formalised on 21 September, while a large village of administration, accommodation and support buildings, including a separate concentration camp, Mittelbau-Dora, sprang up locally and proliferated rapidly in the otherwise largely deserted landscape. Pending sufficient accommodation for the many thousands of slave labourers, some 6,000 were forced to 'live' fulltime, crushed together in the tunnel works, rarely if ever seeing daylight. In addition, the workforce included 5,000 'paid' foreign workers and 500 German weapons specialists, all of whom lived in more tolerable conditions.

Originally Mittelwerk was set the wholly unrealistic target of producing 1,800 V2s per month, and while this was soon halved, it was still a very tall order to assemble the 20,000 components necessary for each, extremely complex V2. After a very poor start in December 1943, when only three V2s left the production line, all of which failed to launch successfully, things improved only very slowly, with many of the fifty produced in January, eighty-six in February and one hundred and seventy in March, also failing to achieve their design performance at launch or in flight.

The story of achievement and horror at Mittelwerk is told in full elsewhere. Achievement there certainly was, ultimately with a massive output of missiles, jet engines and aircraft, although the rate varied constantly, with the state of the war, the resources available and the whims of Herr Hitler – and the cost was very high. The horror was also indisputable, with the conditions for the countless slave labourers indescribable, and with brutal punishments meted out when any sign of poor work or sabotage was suspected. It is right the victims be remembered again in Chapter Thirteen: Requiem.

Back at Peenemünde, rocket trials resumed on 6 October 1943, with a successful launch from Test Stand VII, followed by two failures and another success on 25 October, and continued there at a relatively slow rate, with the first V2 to be built at Mittelwerk detonating three seconds after ignition and failing to lift off on 27 January 1944, setting the trend for many more failures from V2s built there, again leading to suspicions of poor quality control and/or sabotage at the new plant with the inevitable 'witch hunt' and ruthless retribution. Test firings continued at Peenemünde

A V2 being raised from its *Meillerwagen* transport/erector, for a test launch. (Courtesy HTM Peenemünde)

Above and Left: An A4 (V2) rocket being raised from its Miellerwagen transporter/erector. (Courtesy HTM Peenemünde)

Right: Final Checks on an A4 (V2) before launch. (Author, Courtesy HTM Peenemünde)

Below: Test Stand VII at Peenemünde. (Author, Courtesy HTM Peenemünde)

until 20 February 1945, those from new launch pads at Karlshagen and Greifswalder Oie having ceased in November 1944 as the Russians advanced towards them. Additionally, there were five launches from railcars, between 25 November and 4 December, the locations and success rates unknown.

Meanwhile, A4 test firings had got underway at Blizna with the first launch attempted there on 5 November 1943 and two more following by the end of the year, none of which were successful, while only two of the next six firings in January went as planned. In addition to the launch failures, many of the rockets were bursting in the air as they re-entered the earth's atmosphere. By May the launch rate increased markedly with up to four per day, but of the seventy-two that month only ten were successful. The main fault was found to be overheating in critical areas of the rocket and it was hoped that this would be largely rectified by packing all available spaces with glass wool to absorb and disperse the heat. With the Russians now closing in on Blizna, V2 trials ceased there in June 1944 after 204 launches having been attempted, but they continued at a new site in the Tuchola Forest, west of Grudziadz, in northern Poland from 10 September 1944 until 11 January 1945.

An A4 (V2) test launch, location unknown. (Courtesy Medmenham Collection)

Continuing his efforts to get more influence over the two new weapons, Himmler seized his chance in the wake of Operation HYDRA, claiming that only his men were capable of preventing highly classified information on the missiles falling prey to the Allies' agents, as it was believed to have done at Peenemünde. He also believed he could rescue the programme from the constraints of army bureaucracy and, while this appealed to the SS faithful, it seemed to fall on deaf ears among those who mattered. Becoming more extreme, Himmler then launched his 'dirty tricks' campaign against key figures opposing him with trumped up charges against von Braun, his brother, Magnus, Klaus Riedel and others, alleging treason. Specifically, he alleged that Riedel did not want to be associated with a 'murder instrument' and that von Braun was building a spaceship, in which to fly to England with the rocket plans! As a result, several of the rocketeers were incarcerated, until Speer and Dornberger interceded on their behalf and they were set free.

By May 1944 Mittelwerk was producing thirty rockets a day; one front-line army V2 launch battalion had been declared 'operational' and another was not far behind, while the huge bunkers and several tactical sites were nearing completion in the Pas de Calais. At last von Braun felt able to suggest that the rocket campaign against London: Operation PENGUIN could begin in September 1944. To that end, army *Generalleutnant* Eric Heinemann was ordered to prepare LXV Armee Korps (LXV Army Corps) to co-ordinate and support the operations of both missiles, with air force *Oberst* Eugen Walter as his deputy, underlining the joint nature of the headquarters. To Heinemann, this was somewhat of a 'poisoned chalice', with both military services deeply antagonistic to the joint command, with internecine rivalry, fierce competition for increasingly scarce resources rampant and neither weapon ready to deploy.

The failed attempt on Hitler's life in July 1944 led to the replacement of *Generaloberst* Fromm, as head of the *Waffenamt* (Army Ordnance Department), by Himmler, thus giving him the greater influence in the rocket's final development he dearly sought. In August, the *Wehrmacht* responded by creating what was, in effect, a private firm, the Peenemünde Elektromechanische Werk, to be run by the head of Siemens with von Braun as his deputy, reporting directly to the armament ministry. Himmler countered at once, promoting Kammler to *Gruppenführer-SS*, making him responsible for overseeing all aspects of V2 development and deployment, reporting directly to him. Potentially this could make life very difficult for the hard working, long-suffering Dornberger but, in the name of duty and loyalty to his nation, von Braun persuaded him not to resign. Residual trials work on the V2 had now moved from Blizna to Tuchola Forest (code name *Heidekraut*), in Poland.

By the end of August 1944 the Allies were advancing rapidly through north-west France, occupying the best sites for the flying-bomb operations against London, and the huge concrete silos destined for the V2, while causing General Heinemann's LXV Army Corps to retreat into Belgium. Himmler then announced that he was promoting Hans Kammler to *Obergruppenführer-SS* and giving him command of all V2 rocket operations, in Operation PENGUIN, with orders from the Führer to begin

Above and below: Redundant rail link to Baltic coastal test stands. (Author, Courtesy HTM Peenemünde)

firing half the rockets at London, and half at Paris, as soon as they became available. So it was that General Heinemann and his deputy, *Oberst* Walter, ceded operational control of the missiles to the SS, remaining responsible only for such services as intelligence, the prepositioning of weapons and guard duties. At the same time, news came through from *Heidekraut* that Dornberger had finally mastered the airburst problem by riveting a metal sleeve around the fuel tank compartment. Seemingly, the V2 was now ready for war and it was time for Hitler's' final fling'(Chapter Ten).

Similar infighting had been raging within the Luftwaffe, with its political masters and with the German Army. Typically, *Generalfeldmarschall* Erhard Milch, the Luftwaffe's Inspector General and head of the Air Ministry's Technical Office charged with aircraft production, and General Ernst Udet, Director of Research and Development and later Director General of Luftwaffe Equipment, were continually at loggerheads. Both were avowed Nazis, loyal to Hitler and their direct master, Hermann Göring, but neither was known to be a clever strategist or tactician, and the endless debates on the way ahead for the flying bomb were driven as much by politics and personal agendas as by the imperatives of war. While there was dismay in the air force when Göring ordered the cancellation of the German heavy bomber programme, his obsession with numbers arguing that two and a half medium bombers (Heinkel He111, Junkers Ju88 and Dornier Do17) could be produced for the cost of one such bomber, this should have helped prospects for the flying bomb. However, Göring and others within the German hierarchy were against priority treatment for the two missiles; this was reflected in February 1940 dictum that all work should be stopped on new aircraft and associated projects which could not mature and reach the front line within the following twelve months. This seems a very surprising decision, reiterated as late as September 1941, in that it was very much to the detriment of a continued advance of the new German technologies already in train.

Undeterred, and with sensible foresight, the aircraft industry had continued with those military projects which they believed would be needed in the future, as private ventures, and in the flying bomb the gamble paid off. In Berlin, Milch, recognizing that his all-important weapons development programmes could quickly lose its momentum, forged a closer relationship with Albert Speer, who had taken over as Armaments Minister in February 1942; the two realised that the flying bomb, already in an advanced state of design, could be a viable substitute for the heavy bomber. They also believed that, with the RAF's fearsome raid on Lübeck still on his mind,

In this VIP visit to the A4 (V2) Test Stand VII at Peenemünde in 1944, *Generalmajor* Dornberger and *Generaloberst* Fromm (right) escort *Generalfeldmarschall* Keitel (centre) and General Warlimot. (Author, Courtesy HTM Peenemünde)

Hitler would welcome a reminder of the chance to exact revenge in kind with the rocket and flying bomb while, inter alia, raising the Luftwaffe's morale. They argued that the flying bomb would be a sensible adjunct to the Army's V2 rocket, without any great demand on scarce resources, such as precious aviation fuel, the pulse-jet running on standard petrol.

This boded well for Gosslau of Argus and Lusser of Fieseler, the main protagonists of the unmanned flying bomb, who sensed that the time had come for them to submit their optimistic progress report on the tests and trials they had carried out and on their projections for the future. This they did on 28 April 1942, with specific proposals to the *Reichsluftfahrt Ministerium* (RLM), the German Air Ministry, for a cruise missile carrying a half-ton warhead over a range of 186 statute miles at speeds of 435 mph. This was a tall order but the proposal was rushed through the staff channels for the final version to be submitted to the Air Ministry on 5 June and signed off by Milch on 19 June 1942, a mere seven weeks after it had been tabled. Moreover, the project was included in the Luftwaffe's *Vulkanprogram* (Volcano) programme, giving it the priority it needed in the allocation of resources. In Germany, the Fieseler flying bomb would be christened Fi 103, and be known as *Vergeltungswaffe Eins* (V1) (Retaliation Weapon 1), but with the cover name *Flakzielgerät-76* (FZG-76) (anti-aircraft aiming device-76) and nicknamed *Maikäfer* (Maybug), all within Project *Kirschkern* (Cherrystone). To the Allies it would be the V1, the Pilotless Aircraft (PAC), 'FLY', 'Buzz Bomb', 'Doodlebug' or 'Diver'.

With Lusser in charge of the airframe, Gosslau the engine, Guido Wünsch the guidance system and Rheinmetall-Borsig the catapult, work on the V1 then accelerated. The 25-foot fuselage, built of steel sheeting wrapped around and welded to tubular formers, would house the 'brains' of the missile, its short, stub wings, spanning a mere 17 feet 6 inches, were mounted well back, while a standard tailplane, with horizontal stabilisers and fin, was fitted with conventional elevators and rudder, the fin also supporting the pulse-jet engine and its long jet pipe. This was a simple monoplane, resembling a small fighter aircraft. A sophisticated, integrated control system incorporated an autopilot which governed altitude and airspeed, while a weighted pendulum, damped by a stabilized gyrocompass, controlled pitch and roll. Rudder control was sufficient for the limited directional changes required, thus eliminating the need for wing-mounted ailerons. All power requirements, together with pressurization for the fuel tanks, were provided by compressed air stored in two large spherical tanks, resembling giant golf balls. For ground launches, the V1 would be attached to a cradle, to be driven up a 150 feet inclined ramp by a piston in a slotted tube, given an initial thrust of 66,000 pounds by steam generated in a combustion chamber containing a mixture of hydrogen peroxide (*T-Stoff*) and sodium or potassium permanganate *(Z-Stoff)*. When reaching flying speed, the pulse jet would take over and the cradle would detach and fall away.

The first V1 airframe was delivered to Peenemünde on 30 August 1942, only two months after Milch had given the go-ahead for Project Cherrystone, and static tests began two days later. These tests, and others carried out in the Hermann Göring Wind Tunnel at Braunschweig-Volkenrode Aeronautical Institute, revealed that the pulse jet stalled at high speeds and generated excessive vibration, also that thrust decreased with increases in speed. With these defects believed remedied, the first ground launch of a V1 took place on 24 December 1942, the tiny aeroplane riding up the ramp on its sled and into the air correctly, the engine starting and separation from the sled taking place as planned. While this first flight lasted less than a minute, the embryo missile achieved a speed of 310 mph and the test was deemed to have been a great success, generating much needed confidence in the project and resulting in the formation of an *Arbeitsstab* FZG-76 (a V1 Project Team), which included Gosslau and Lusser, to supervise the missile's development and production.

With confidence now high, Hitler, Göring and Himmler were invited to Peenemünde again in January 1943 where they witnessed a faultless launch, after which the missile veered off to the right and crashed – as it had in previous tests. The project team was nonplussed but the diminutive test pilot Hanna Reitsch came to the rescue by offering to fly the V1 to evaluate the problem, if it could be fitted with a cockpit and basic controls. This was quite practicable, and while there were grave concerns within the Nazi hierarchy, and Hitler himself, over the dangers inherent in such a hazardous initiative, the desire to solve the problem eventually prevailed, and on Hanna's fourth test flight in the re-configured aircraft, the cause of the problem was revealed. It had become clear that the steam-driven sled was unable to withstand the shock of the catapult launch, one or more bolts shearing and causing the wings to flutter at a crucial stage in the launch. Stronger bolts were fitted and the trials resumed with such success that full production began in May 1943.

By the end of July 1943, eighty-four launches had been attempted, of which sixteen were dropped from a 'mother' aircraft, and sixty-eight catapulted from the ground, but only twenty-eight of the latter going to plan. Other than the defective launches, the main cause of the failures was the disintegration of the airstream inlet shutters which, in any event were only expected to function correctly for the one flight planned for each missile. There was some good news, however, one V1 achieving a speed of 390 mph and another a range of 140 miles, close to the performance figures predicted. Significantly, none of these test flights carried guidance equipment, and none were carried out at the maximum operational weight. Inevitably, the 'blame-game' for all the failures was in full swing but there was general agreement that the rush to get the missile operational had led to inadequate tests of critical components and analysis of the failures.

When it was believed that the causes of all these failures had been found and remedied, fully-loaded V1s were put through their paces with the Askania guidance system fitted to operate the flight controls, using compressed air to ensure that the directional gyroscope remained aligned with, or returned to alignment with, the pre-set magnetic compass. At pre-planned ranges, small explosive charges opened spoilers on the horizontal stabilizer to tip the missile into a dive on to the target. However, no way had been found of compensating for high crosswinds and the use of mechanical rather than electrical range counters were insufficiently accurate to render the V1 a precision weapon.

The date for deploying the weapons to their launch sites in the Pas de Calais, set for December 1943, was very much at risk. Fieseler in Kassel could not generate the number of bombs required, and a second production facility coming on line at Volkswagen's Fallerslaben factory was not able to make up the deficit, the total output falling well short of the 50,000 units per month, demanded by Göring. An initial command structure was in place, with *Oberst* Max Wachtel appointed commander of *Lehr-und Erprobungskommando-V* (a V1 test and training facility), at Zamplin, conveniently close to Peenemünde, and it would be he who had the unenviable task of explaining why the demands of the leadership could not be met in the timescales specified. A suitable workforce was proving hard to find, only 65 per cent of that needed, fully trained, was expected to be available by the end of July 1943, with increased Allied bombing demanding additional manpower to build up the fighter force, while the V2 rocket team seemed to be getting more than their fair share of what was on offer. Moreover, there was insufficient ground support equipment and many of the V1s arriving at the new training unit were found to be defective or without essential components, 60 per cent of those declared ready for use failing to launch correctly or to perform as required in flight.

The obvious vulnerability of Peenemünde to Allied bombing, led to the construction of another launch and training facility at Brüsterort, north of Königsberg, and it was there that *Flak-Regiment 155(W)* (Flak Regiment 155(W)), the first of the V1's operational units, began its training on 1 September 1943, the first V1 being launched from there later that month. The initial V1 output at Fallersleben was two units per day, far below the basic training requirement of 6 per day, and there was no possibility of 155(W) completing its training by the target date of 1 October. Milch, however, still believing that the flying bomb would eventually alter the course of the war, and that Londoners would not be able to withstand a bombardment of one bomb every twelve minutes, kept up the pressure and, notionally, Flak Regiment 155(W) did become 'operational' in October 1943, firing its first missile later that month. While this did not tell the whole story, it would be fair to say that the regiment, although still lacking critical items of equipment and specialist manpower, when it moved to northern France shortly thereafter, did pave the way for the V1 'Doodlebug' to go to war (See Chapter Five).

Arguably not one of Hitler's 'retaliation' weapons, in that it could not threaten England, RMB's *Rheinbote* deserves a mention, because it made use of technologies developed for the Aggregate rockets, and did affect the battles as the Allies advanced into Europe. Testing this multi-stage, solid-fuel, long-range artillery rocket began at the firm's weapons range at Leba, in the Gdansk region of Poland, in 1941, with ten launches stretching over a full year. The first three stages of the rocket were tested independently before all four were launched together, culminating in April 1943 in a very successful demonstration before a VIP audience, which included the head of rocket development in the *HWA*, General Schneider. This secured official approval for further tests but without granting the priorities in materials it needed, the shortages only being resolved when the project officer, Lieutenant Colonel Alfred Tröller, 'buried' the extra requirements within the whole *Vergeltingswaffen* programme, hinting darkly that the SS were becoming interested in the project. Perhaps it was as a result of this ominous suggestion that the *Wehrmacht* was quick to authorise the supply of propulsion powder and metal necessary for the immediate production of 200 *Rheinbote*, at RMB's Berlin-Marienfelde factory. The test programme then encountered further problems with repetitious airbursts attributed to inconsistent burning in the fourth stage combustion chamber, while the fins tended to break off at supersonic speeds. Both problems having been remedied, further demonstrations took place at Leba on 15 November 1943, before another select group of VIPs, now including

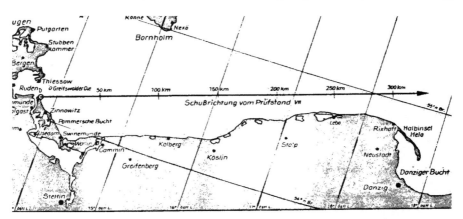

Fi 103 (V1) Baltic Air Weapons range, off Pomerania. (Author, Courtesy HTM Peenemünde)

Above and below: The original offices and workshops on the southern edge of Flugplatz Peenemünde, where the Fi 103s were prepared for the flight trials. (Author)

Steam Generator, to power piston in launching Fi 103. (Author, Courtesy IWM Duxford)

Gruppenführer-SS Kammler and *Generalmajor* Dornberger, this time with mixed results. The first three rounds achieved ranges in excess of ninety-three miles, but with some disappointment at the limited effects of the small warhead, while the fourth broke up after launch, causing panic among the onlookers. As a result, Dornberger recommended that further work on the weapon cease forthwith but he was overruled by Kammler who ordered the rocket gun to be deployed for immediate use on the front line, and allocated the necessary resources to that end.

This was not the end of the trials. Tröller and the RMB specialists continued to work hard to increase the reliability of the rocket, its performance and effectiveness, using the range at Leba and at Waldheim (re-named Drogoslaw), close to the V2 test range at Tucheler Heide, in Poland. Improvements came slowly, ranges increasing to 118 miles, and craters now measuring 11 feet (3.3 metres) in diameter and 4 feet (1.2 metres) deep, with greater destruction all round. However, the rocket was still unreliable, ignition between the stages remaining one of the main problems. Of Kammler's initial order of 300 projectiles, only 115 had been delivered by the end of 1944, with the promise of 222 by the end of January 1945. Meanwhile, all the necessary support facilities were prepared, often by innovation or improvisation, typically with the V2's *Meillerwagen* being modified for the rocket's transportation and erection and, by the end of 1944, sufficient firing teams had been trained for the tactical deployment of one battery of *Artillerie-Abteilung 709* (*Artillery Regiment 709*) – and so the *Rheinbote* went to war.

Above and right: Fi 103 launch sites, between Flugplatz Peenemünde and Baltic coast. (Author, Courtesy HTM Peenemünde)

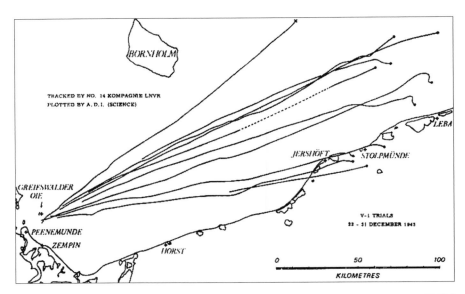

Fi 103 (V1) tracks over Baltic range, pre-modification. (Author, Courtesy HTM Peenemünde)

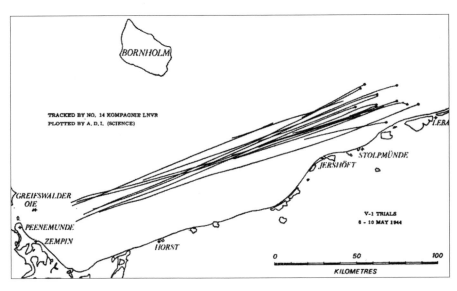

Fi 103 (V1) tracks over Baltic range, post-modification. (Author, Courtesy HTM Peenemünde)

Chapter 4

No Hiding Place

It was perhaps surprising that Allied intelligence agencies were a little slow in recognising fully or accepting the sinister dangers that were lurking within the German scientific, technological, armament and military communities during the 1930s, as that nation began to circumvent or ignore, quite openly, the constraints imposed at Versailles. There was little attempt to conceal the rocketeers' work at Kummersdorf, but only the naive could have believed that, as the Nazi movement gathered strength, this was solely to do with space exploration, and they could surely not have missed the significance of the HVA's move from Kummersdorf to the huge new, highly classified facility at Peenemünde, which began in 1937. There seem to be several reasons why Britain was slow to react to tell-tale signs of these threats, one being a high degree of scepticism at the top, that if Britain had yet to make progress in the field of rocketry how could the Germans be so far ahead? Then there were those who thought that significant information which came their way, some almost incidentally, or was offered to them on a plate, was 'misinformation' deliberately 'planted', a ruse to mislead and distract. Also, there were those who thought they should be given the lead in seeking the truth, but were not, and conversely others who hesitated to become involved lest the search for the new airborne weapons being hinted at turned out to be a wild goose chase. All this scepticism and lack of definitive intelligence, examples of which follow below, led to procrastination and serious, perhaps near crucial, delays in responding to the threats inherent in the weapons which did materialise, eventually allowing German innovation to cause such havoc among the Allies in the closing stages of the war.

The sources of information on the burgeoning German interest in military rockets were many and various, but fell largely into three categories, each with its own particular value in content and timing. There was human intelligence, 'HUMINT', derived from diplomatic exchanges, spies, friendly agents, random documents or simply conversations overheard, typically at prisoner of war (PoW) centres, 'bugged' for the purpose. Then there was 'SIGINT' the interception of radio signals at many listening posts, particularly from the highly-secret Government Code and Cypher School (GC & CS), at Bletchley Park. If considered potentially useful, every effort would be made to validate their authenticity and dispense with deliberate, inherently harmful misinformation before such inputs were analysed, collated and passed to relevant 'customers', or stored for future reference.

The third major source of invaluable information, often triggered by HUMINT or SIGINT, was air reconnaissance, in three primary forms: Photographic Recce (PR), Fighter Recce (FR) and Visual Recce (Vis Recce). PR aircraft, typically RAF Spitfires and Mosquitos, together with a variety of USAAF aircraft, usually operating singly at high or medium levels (when cloud cover allowed), using vertical or oblique cameras for mapping, area cover and pinpoint photography. These aircraft were stripped of all equipment not vital to the role, such as weapons, to enable them to fly as high and as fast as possible, thereby giving them some immunity against enemy fighters and anti-aircraft guns.

FR aircraft, such as the RAF Spitfires and Mustangs and USAAF P-38 Lightnings, were high-performance fighters, equipped with cameras optimised for low-level oblique photography; for their survival, they relied on surprise, high speed, manoeuvrability, tactical routing – and (for those suitably equipped) their guns. The retention of weapons also allowed them, if authorised, to attack high value targets of opportunity – but rarely at the expense of their primary role, that of gleaning detail of the assigned or opportunity targets, visually and with close-range oblique photography. Incidentally, all military pilots, whatever their role, were expected to report sightings of potential targets, or indeed any other information which might be of use to intelligence staffs, throughout their sorties.

Until 1939 PR had been the responsibility of the Special Intelligence Service (SIS) within MI5, its rapid development driven by such men as Squadron Leaders F.C.V. Laws, a PR veteran of the Royal Flying Corps (RFC), and W.H.G. Heath at the Air Ministry, P.J.A. Riddell of Bomber Command, and a freelance civilian aerial photographer, Frederick Sidney Cotton. They laid the foundations for a small photographic interpretation (PI) section, comprising three officers, who draw information from PR sorties flown by Blenheim, Hudson, Lockheed 12A and, latterly, Spitfire aircraft, operating covertly from RAF Heston, under the cover name of No.2 Camouflage Unit. In January 1940 this became the Photographic Development Unit (PDU), and six months later the Photographic Reconnaissance Unit (PRU), under the operational control of Coastal Command, evolving into a number of

Spitfire flights, based at different locations in the UK until, at the end of 1940, No.1 PRU took up residence at RAF Benson, Oxfordshire, where it remained throughout the war. Information gathered by aircrew operating far into the continent of Europe went first to the Photographic Interpretation Unit (PIU), which started life at Wembley before moving to the more spacious Danesfield House, Medmenham, in April 1941, where it became the Central Interpretation Unit (CIU). There it was analysed and collated before being presented to intelligence staffs and, where appropriate, to the relevant battle managers.

Head of the Technical Control Section of CIU was Wing Commander Douglas Kendall, a pre-war aerial survey pilot, who held the highest security clearance and had access to all intelligence sources. From the start the CIU nurtured a rapidly increasing band of PIs and reprographic staff at Medmenham and model-makers at Phyllis Court, Henley. Inevitably, the CIU became deeply involved in the search for definitive evidence of German rockets and flying bombs, their trials, production centres, and deployment sites. The CIU continued to expand rapidly as the war progressed, absorbing the Bomber Command Damage Assessment Section and the Night Photographic Interpretation Section of No.3 PRU, at RAF Oakington, and, as more Americans joined the staff, the CIU became the Allied Central Interpretation Unit (ACIU) on 1 May 1944. At peak strength 1,700 personnel served at Medmenham, sifting through a daily input of 25,000 negatives and 60,000 prints, and by 1945 the ACIU had generated a library of 5,000,000 prints and 40,000 reports. This was big business – and it paid off.

This chapter will deal later with the many invaluable contributions made by the aircrew and ground specialists involved in wartime air reconnaissance, in discovering the *Vergeltungswaffen* and in the ensuing campaign against them. First, however, it would be instructive to review the many diverse inputs on the two weapons and how they were dealt with by the hierarchy in the British scientific and technical communities in what became a protracted, often fractious, debate on the feasibility of the technology alluded to and the validity of the intelligence derived.

The author could find no record of London reacting positively to clues relating to work on offensive rockets underway at Kummersdorf throughout the 1930s, but the intense activity at Peenemünde in the second half of the decade could surely not have gone unnoticed, especially when so much effort was devoted to the site's security. In his 19 September 1939 speech at Danzig, Hitler himself hinted openly that Germany was developing weapons with which they themselves could not be attacked. Then, in early November 1939, came the 'Oslo Report', in which British intelligence staffs were offered details of the evolutionary work by German scientists on radar, magnetic mines and the new aerial weapons being developed at Kummersdorf and Peenemünde. The report, written by the disillusioned German mathematician and physicist, Hans Ferdinand Mayer, came in a package which included a small glass tube, contents unknown, but part of a prototype proximity fuse. It seems that the information therein was largely discounted by many in London, as an elaborate hoax designed to mislead the Allies.

From the start of the war a sporadic stream of information began to emerge from Poles forced to work at Peenemünde, and later from the Polish Underground at various locations, with one partisan reporting a conversation with a drunken German airman in Königsberg, who boasted that Germany had a new weapon, which would 'conquer the world'. This information was passed to Warsaw and on to London, which requested further investigations by the Poles embedded at Peenemünde. This elicited the information from Polish 'volunteers' for latrine duty who, in their wanderings with impunity abound the camp, confirmed the presence there of a 'small, pilotless aeroplane'. Other occupied countries also contributed; Major V.L.U. Glyth, Royal Danish Army, secreted a parcel of information on to the last diplomatic train to leave Copenhagen at the start of the German occupation which contained details of the latest German dispositions in the country. He continued to pass intelligence to the British, primarily via Danish seamen and a clandestine radio network throughout the war and, by the winter of 1942/43, his inputs were containing strong evidence of intensive rocket and flying bomb activity at Peenemünde.

Neutral countries also became involved. In December 1942 the SIS Station Chief in the Stockholm office reported a conversation overheard by a new agent, Aage Andreasen, a neutral armaments engineer, in a Berlin restaurant between Professor Fauner, of the Berlin Technische Hochschule, and a German weapons engineer, Stephan Szenassy, concerning a rocket that was being developed with a range of 200 kilometres, a warhead of 5 tons and an automatic steering system. This caught the eye of R.V. Jones, who was now both the scientific adviser to the SIS and Assistant Director Intelligence Science (ADI Science) at the Air Ministry. Dr Reginald Victor ('RV') Jones had left Oxford with a first-class honours degree in physics, joined the Royal Aeroplane Establishment in 1936 and the Directorate of Scientific Intelligence in the Air Ministry in 1939 and became a very

Danesfield House, Second World War home of the Central Interpretation Unit (CIU). (Author)

significant player in the fractious debate on the two missiles. Then, in January 1943, another agent from Sweden confirmed the activity at Peenemünde, specifically that rockets were being tested there and that a large airfield was also being constructed on the north-east corner of the Usedom, all of which were then featured in the SIS Digest, dated 8 February 1943. Such reports, seen by the appropriate departments in the SIS and the War Office, were now coming in thick and fast, and could not be ignored.

In London Professor Lindemann, who had been raised to the peerage in 1941 to become Lord Cherwell, was Prime Minister Churchill's Chief Scientific Adviser throughout the war. A somewhat haughty, self-opinionated but well-educated physicist, Cherwell had studied in Germany at Darmstadt and Berlin universities; he denounced much of the evidence on offer, suggesting that the 'long, cylindrical objects' photographed at Peenemünde were no more than 'some sort of balloon'. He and Dr A.D. Crow, the chief rocket expert at the Ministry of Supply, claimed that the rocket envisaged would have to be powered by solid fuel, most probably cordite, because the technology which would allow the use of liquid fuel had yet to be developed and that, therefore, the missile would be far too heavy to reach London from launch sites on the continent. Nor did he believe that the Germans had the expertise to produce an effective flying bomb, able to threaten the British capital. His friend, R.V. Jones thought otherwise but, to his dismay, little immediate action was being taken to follow up on all the foregoing leads, including the Oslo report, at least until a further piece of HUMINT emerged on 22 March 1943. This came from Squadron Leader Denys Felkin, who listened in to a 'bugged' conversation between two German generals, General Ritter von Thoma and General Ludwig Crüwell, at the Trent House PoW camp at Cockfosters, in North London. There, von Thoma recalled seeing rockets at Peenemünde, some eighteen months before, which were said to be nearing operational status – and wondered why they were not raining down on London already.

This steady accumulation of intelligence finally convinced the War Office that the Chiefs of Staff should be advised of the potential threats, and this was done in a consolidated report on 11 April 1943. They in turn believed Churchill should be informed, and that a single individual should head a review of all available evidence on the missiles which now had to be anticipated, and so it was that, on 20 April 1943, Major Duncan

German rocket and flying bomb research and production units. (Author, Courtesy HTM Peenemünde)

Sandys was called on to head comprehensive studies of German long-range rocket developments. His remit included the identification of the weapons, how they were powered, controlled and launched, where they were being produced, tested and likely to be deployed, concentrating on an area of the continent within 130 miles of London and Southampton. All intelligence sources would be made available to him and his investigations accorded the highest priority.

Duncan Sandys MP became Financial Secretary to the War Office in 1941, following service as an artillery officer with the British Expeditionary Force in 1940. Thereafter, he was involved in operational evaluations of anti-aircraft rockets until released from active duty after a traffic accident. He was favoured by Prime Minister Winston Churchill (his father-in-law) but not by Lord Cherwell, whose preference for this important appointment had been R. V. Jones. This did nothing to deter Sandys from getting on with the job he had been given, assisted by an old friend and military adviser, Colonel Ken Post, the two working hard to get to the truth on the rocket and flying bomb, and how best to defend against them. They began by enlisting the help of the Joint Intelligence Committee (JIC), which comprised the intelligence heads of the three services, under a permanent chairman from the Foreign Office. Also, they took guidance from the SIS on the likely validity of the relevant intelligence gathered so far and welcomed help from MI10, the Military Intelligence Germany (Technical) Branch, and the PoW section. The CIU at Medmenham was tasked to review all the photographs of north-west France, within a 130 mile radius of London, looking for any evidence of long-range gun emplacements, flying-bomb or rocket launch sites and, where cover was lacking, request the PRU be tasked to fill in the gaps. Two new cells were set up at the CIU, one to deal with Peenemünde, under the eyes of the RAF PI, Flight Lieutenant André Kenny, the second covering north-west France run by the Army PI, Captain Robert Rowell. With such inbuilt tensions at the top, it would not have been surprising if some critical, 'raw' information had failed to flow freely in all directions.

In the War Office Dr Charles Frank and Captain Matthew Pryor, of MI14, which dealt with German military matters, had taken an unofficial short-cut to have the existing photography of Peenemünde checked again, and requested additional cover as a matter of urgency. Photographs taken on 19 January 1943 were inconclusive, with snow covering much of the area, but another on 1 March showed interesting developments around the three circular revetments at the north-western tip of the Usedom peninsula, including the recent construction of several buildings similar to those being built in the coastal regions of France, the most likely area for launching missiles against London. This prompted the every persistent Pryor to call for new photo coverage of these areas, looking specifically for some sort of launching ramps, but nothing definite was found, and Medmenham concluded that, while there was no positive evidence that rockets and/or flying bombs were going to be launched from there, neither was there any evidence that they would not be!

There seems to have been some uncertainty within RAF circles as to the part they should be playing in this saga; assuming that the rocket was merely an extension to Germany's long-range artillery, it was surely of more interest to the army and airmen should, therefore, limit their involvement to a 'watching brief'. As for the Americans, the archives show that information on Peenemünde was passed to a senior US official, Allen Dulles, in May, but it may be that they were not given the full picture on the possible threat to England and to the huge Allied invasion fleet mustering around the Channel ports, despite the contribution which the USAAF's 8th and 9th Air Forces could make against the missile development, production and launch sites. Such an early opportunity to do so arose that month, when agents and PR revealed what could only be a launch site for V2s at Watten, in the Pas-de-Calais.

In April 1943 Bletchley Park had reported signals indicating that 14 and 15 Companies of the *Luftnachrichten-Regiment* (a German Experimental Air Signals Regiment) had deployed *Würzburg G* tracking radars to Rügen Island, Bornholm and several other locations along the Baltic coast to the east, which had been pinpointed, and which, together with reports from agents operating in the area, suggested forthcoming trials with 'pilotless aircraft'. The first real 'coup' came on 22 April 1943 when the crew of a PR Mosquito, returning from a bomb damage assessment (BDA) sortie over Stettin, left their vertical cameras running as they flew home along the Baltic coast and over Peenemünde. From the photographs, the PIs at the CIU spotted an unusual object, some 25 feet long, shrouded in steam, with flames issuing from one end – which was no longer there on photographs taken 4 seconds later, leading them to assume that there had been a rocket of sorts launched there. Usedom was now being photographed by Mosquitos twice a week, those prints on 12 June revealing a 35 feet high, 'white-ish' cylinder, some 5 feet in diameter, with three fins at the tail end, very similar to objects photographed on rail trucks accompanied by fuel tankers. Throughout that month intelligence from Peenemünde continued to come in thick and fast, typically from agents such as the 'Famille Martin' in Luxembourg, the Frenchman Leon Henri Roth, and foreign workers accommodated in the Usedom's Trassenheide camp – all pointing to the development of large rockets, with assembly units, launch pits and towers. More evidence came from a disgruntled Luftwaffe weapons officer who reported seeing 'winged missiles' and associated catapults at Peenemünde, supporting the notion of flying bombs. Finally, on 23 June, a Mosquito from 540 Squadron photographed two V2s, leaving Flight Lieutenant Kenny at the CIU in no doubt about the rockets. Duncan Sandys thought likewise, and despite Lord Cherwell's continued scepticism, he recommended the earliest heaviest possible bombing of Peenemünde.

On 29 June 1943 Churchill and the Cabinet agreed and plans were laid for a precision raid by all available aircraft from RAF Bomber Command, to take place on the night of 17/18 August, in Operation HYDRA (See Chapter Eight). Their decision was vindicated when, on 16 August, a comprehensive dossier on weapons development at Peenemünde was acquired by the French agent Léon Faye and flown to England in an RAF Lysander of the Special Operations Squadron.

Post-Operation HYDRA the War Office called for more details on the weapons, ideally from human sources on the ground, despite security at Peenemünde having been tightened, and from those survivors of HYDRA who were then transferred to a new weapons range in Poland. Some V2 development work continued at Peenemünde, but the next test flight did not take place until seven weeks later. The Germans attempted to deceive the Allies by faking bomb damage there with black and white lines painted to simulate charred beams and dummy craters, all suggesting that the raid was far more successful than it was, thereby hoping to deter further raids, but the well-rehearsed PIs at the CIU were not fooled. There was no hiding place.

At 13.05 on 22 August a V1, rumoured to have been air launched, fell on the Danish island of Bornholm. It was with great courage and presence of mind that a group of Danes, led by Hasager Christiansen, beat the *Wehrmacht* to the site by some fifteen minutes, enabling them to photograph major parts of the airframe, the automatic pilot and compressed air spheres, and gather brief but near-accurate details of the inert bomb, which were then rushed to London. The Gestapo suspected the Danish officers Lieutenant Colonel Christiansen, Major Glyth and Colonel Nordentoft and there began a dangerous game of cat and mouse to avoid their arrest, incarceration or worse. Christiansen alone was caught and suffered grievously in German hands, but the details the group had gleaned gave the V1 a new priority, *vis*

Left: Now you see it, now you don't. Early sighting of an A4 (V2) rocket on Test Stand VII, at the north-east point of the Peenemünde Peninsula. (Medmenham Collection)

Below: Vertical photograph of Test Stand XI, in the centre of the Peenemünde peninsula, used primarily for rocket engine tests. (Medmenham Collection)

vis the V2, convincing the doubters that the flying bomb threat was real and imminent. Lord Cherwell, however, still demurred, claiming that the design was not technically sound and that, with only a 1,000lb warhead, it was no more than an expensive toy, posing no great threat to London. Time would tell.

The debate continued, with a paper circulated on 19 September 1943 outlining what was known to date, seeking the views of specialists on the technological feasibilies of the V2, and more specifically how it might be fuelled to achieve the ranges postulated. Responding to this on 11 October, the eminent scientist

V1 FLYING BOMB ON LAUNCHING RAMP

This photograph, taken by Sqn Ldr John Merifield on 28 November 1943 and interpreted by Flt Lt G B Reynolds, provided the link between Peenemünde and the launch sites in France and finally proved that the 'ski sites' were for launching flying bombs.

One of the first PR photographs of an Fi 103 (V1) Flying Bomb, on the Baltic coast north-east of *Flugplatz* Peenemünde. (Medmenham Collection)

Isaac Lubbock, of the Asiatic Petroleum Company, supported by Colonel Post (Sandys' scientific adviser), believed that the Germans might have come up with a practicable solution for feeding liquid fuel into the combustion chamber using a centrifugal pump, which could double the range of a rocket of comparable weight and warhead using solid fuel. The Projectile Development Establishment at Fort Halstead concurred, at a time when intelligence sources were suggested that 500 of the missiles might have been constructed already, and that a rocket offensive might begin as early as November 1943. Predictably, Lord Cherwell, and his scientific supporter, Dr A.D. Crow, refuted the claim, Cherwell assuring a high-level meeting in the Cabinet Room on 25 October that, if such a weapon did exist, it would be a year before it became operational, repeating that the 'rocket like' objects photographed at Peenemünde were most likely 'some sort of kite balloon' or an 'outsize mortar' and that the rocket postulated was no more than a 'mare's nest', words he would come to regret.

By the autumn of 1943 some fifty PR sorties had been mounted against Peenemünde itself, within a total Allied photographic coverage of 7,500 square miles of enemy territory, and the production of four million prints. Also, useful intelligence inputs from agents and partisans were increasing exponentially, especially in the west coast areas of France where a massive construction programme of V1 and V2 launch sites involved civilian and slave labour. It was on 28 September that the CIU reported what they thought was an underground V1/V2 launch site, at Marquise-Mimoyecques, again in the Pas-de-Calais, and well within the suspected range of the rockets – but they would be in for another unpleasant surprise (Chapter Nine).

It was no surprise when, in the wake of HYDRA, the Germans moved most of their V1 and V2 trials work to Blizna, beyond the effective range of Allied bombers, if not the PR aircraft, and built new production sites below ground where PR could not see them nor bombs reach them, leaving only the tunnel entrances and rail spurs visible and vulnerable. So it was that HUMINT from the Polish Underground and courageous workers producing the weapons became the primary source of information from such new locations as that in the Austrian Alps, south of Salzburg, the Thuringia mountains, Friedrichshafen, Dernau-Marienthal (near Bonn) and, above all, at Mittelwerk. One production unit which could be attacked, on good HUMINT from agents in Bern, Switzerland, and a Luftwaffe informant, was the Gerhard Fieseler factory at Bettenhausen, an eastern suburb of Kassel, where V1s were being produced, and on 22/23 October 1943, RAF bombers obliterated much of Kassel, severely delaying the production and final trials of vital components of the V1 for 'three or four months'.

However, by far the most important production centre for both the V1 and V2, at Mittelwerk, lay deep underground in the Kohnstein mountains, just north of Nordhausen. Other than the tell-tale tunnel entrances and the rail lines leading to them, there was little evidence of the intensive activity in the labyrinth of corridors and caves underground where most of the missiles were being built. Intelligence sources were understandably limited to a few courageous agents and slave labourers working therein, who were either living and dying where they worked, or in little better conditions in the adjacent concentration camp at Mittelbau-Dora - with their replacements for them readily available from the notorious concentration camp at nearby Buchenwald.

In the autumn of 1943 the French Réseau AGIR Resistance Group, in which the French commercial traveller Michel Hollard was a major player with the ways and means of getting into Switzerland undetected, passed invaluable information to the British SIS, without the use of radio, giving the locations of six flying-bomb launch sites. The package showed standard site layouts, albeit adjusted to fit in with the local topography, giving details of 'Maison R' the non-magnetic building necessary for setting up the guidance system of the flying bomb, and a long, thin shed, with a blast-reducing curve at one end which would transpire to be storage facilities for V1s, without wings – this giving rise to the name 'Bois Carré ski site'. With commendable reaction, a PR sortie was launched against one such site at Yvrench, to test the authenticity of this 'scoop'. Sure enough, the photographs gave the necessary confirmation, together with additional information on what appeared to be mountings for a launch ramp, some 150 feet long, pointing at London. Where there was doubt before, there was none now: these were not rocket sites; they were clearly destined for flying bombs.

With the debate on whether and or how to anticipate German missile attacks continuing, an exasperated Churchill decreed that further discussion on scientific theory was pointless and appointed Sir Stafford Cripps, a senior left-wing politician in the coalition government and Minister of Aircraft Production in the War Cabinet, to carry out a full appreciation of the threats and their likely timings. At the inaugural meeting on 8 November1943 the senior PI at Medmenham, Douglas Kendall, updated information on the huge concrete structures at Watten and Wizernes, and at the following meeting R.V. Jones gave his estimates of the range, speed, height and accuracy of the flying bomb. From the abundance of evidence placed before him, Cripps had every reason to conclude that the V1s and V2s did exist and that multiple launch sites were being prepared for them in western France, but he did not think that such an offensive would begin before January 1944. There was no surprise when he recommended that full PR cover of the French sites continue, and that they be bombed whenever and wherever they were found. On 11 November the Chiefs of Staff decreed that Sandys should relinquish his role, and that the JIC should take the lead in evaluating all intelligence pertaining to the two missiles, but with Sandys continuing to sit on the committee and with some of his staff transferred to the JIC. The second Cripps report, dated 17 November, added little, other than revealing the discovery of a third, rather different, bunker being built under the hills at Mimoyecques, Pas de Calais.

Initially, the campaign to be waged against all aspects of the German long-range weapons threat was given the code name BODYLINE, renamed CROSSBOW on 15 November, with all associated targets known as 'Noball' targets, and the collection of intelligence, particularly by PR, an integral part. By the end of November ninety-six 'ski sites' had been discovered, and they would be kept under continuous surveillance thereafter. The Crossbow Committee was formed on 29 December, and met first on 6 January, under the chairmanship of General Stephen Henry, of the New Developments

Division; but still there appears to have been some uncertainty as to whether all these discoveries were valid targets or decoys. However, the evidence was strong enough to convince the realists of the imminence of rocket and flying-bomb attacks against London, and perhaps the invasion ports that, in December 1943, the RAF and USAAF were ordered to begin a strong offensive against the ski sites in France. This coincided with a report from a reliable agent in France, Jeannie Rousseau, that a V1 launch and support unit, Flak Regiment 155W, had arrived at Creil, north of Paris.

Flight Officer Constance Babington-Smith, who had been among the first to notice unusual activity at Peenemünde and its environs, was in the news again at the end of 1943 when she discovered, from archive photographs, what she thought was a tiny aircraft on a launching ramp in the sand dunes at the end of a road to the north of Peenemünde airfield and brought this to the attention of Douglas Kendall. Kendall immediately ordered a review of all previous photographs of the area, plus new cover, and his intuition paid off. On 28 November 1943 a midget aircraft was photographed in the same place by Squadron Leader Merrifield and Flying Officer Whalley, together with identical ramps at Zempin and Zinnowitz, farther along the Baltic coast to the east, which Babington-Smith found replicated and proliferating along the coast of north-west France.

Bletchley Park was also on the case, taking particular interest in SIGINT originating from units and radar tracking stations on the Baltic coast. Such words as 'departure and impact', 'angle-shots', 'explosive trials', and even repeated demands for soap, enabling identification of new units and the work they were undertaking. Decoded signals listing bearings, height and distances could surely mean only that missiles were being launched from Zempin. In November 1943, Bletchley had also intercepted a seemingly innocuous message from Greifswalder Oie which reported the death there of a Luftwaffe radar technician, *Bergefreiter* Wilde, apparently from suicide. The Ultra-wise heads at Bletchley Park wondered why an airman with his qualifications should be at Oie, which had not been of any military interest to them before, so they kept a listening watch on the frequencies being used, noting all the foibles and habits of the operators there as the message traffic increased in significance. Oie was, indeed, going to play a significant part in the rocket and flying-bomb trials to come.

The next few months were relatively and suspiciously quiet on the missile story, causing Section 3G(N) at Bletchley Park to redouble its efforts by introducing a keyword-alerting system, a complicated system understood by few, which looked into the roles of little-known units in the areas of interest.

They included mundane administrative matters, such as stores requisitions, sick reports *et al*, but above all it was the increase in signals traffic between units deployed to the troop exercise area at Blizna which concentrated minds in the intelligence community. The Polish partisans around Blizna added much to these reports, noting that heavy plant moving into the area was believed to be associated with both the rocket and the flying bomb. One agent there found a heavily guarded rail flatbed near Blizna, carrying 'an object which, though covered by a tarpaulin, bore every evidence of an aerial torpedo', but another was more specific assessing the rocket to be some 12 to 14 metres long, about one metre in diameter and perhaps weighing 7 to 12 tons. Importantly, another confirmed that Experimental Battery 444 had been firing V2s at Blizna since November and, significantly in May 1944, came a report that a mobile artillery detachment, believed to be destined for Wizernes (France), had begun training there.

The Americans were now getting impatient for better information on the missiles, and Churchill's Chief Military Assistant, General Ismay, directed that they be brought fully up-to-date on the potential missile threat, and the Crossbow Committee gave them the full story in January 1944. The Americans' reaction was impressive, with the immediate construction of a full-scale replica of the ski sites found in France, for target evaluation and to assist their bomber crews with their forthcoming efforts to destroy them.

With the V1 ski sites now suffering severely from the CROSSBOW offensive, it was not surprising that alternative V1 launch sites were appearing, using mobile, pre-fabricated steel launch ramps, semi-camouflaged in harmony with the natural environment, in what would become known as 'modified sites', the first of these being photographed at Belhamelin, near Cherbourg on 26 April 1944. To further enhance security at these sites, German contractors were now replacing the French, thereby denying this source of intelligence from 'embedded' informants. These tactical sites would be supplied from large, underground storage facilities, such as those at the Nucourt limestone Caves, St-Leu-d'Esserent mushroom caves and the Rilly-la-Montagne rail tunnel. In April, General Eisenhower, the Allied supreme commander, allocated the highest priority to CROSSBOW targets.

Also in April came the first definitive information that the caves at Mittelwerk were producing V2s, when two Polish labourers at the Mittelbau-Dora Concentration Camp spotted a train carrying six rockets and as assortment of launch equipment from the underground plant.

Important discoveries were continuing to be made along the coastal areas of Western France, where a growing strip of ski sites had been identified,

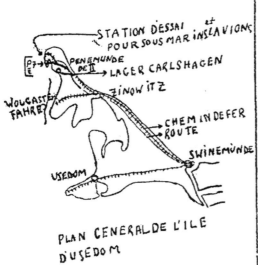

ATELIER DE FABRICATION
ET D'EXPERIMENTATION DE
L'OBUS A FUSÉE.
SE TROUVE A P?... EN PARTIE
SUR TERRE, EN PARTI SOUS-
TERRAIN
FUSÉE EN VOL = LONGUEUR
DE 10 METRES. ELLE EST
VISIBLE PENDANT LE
VOL. ASPECT EN CIGARE.
GARDE SA DROITE. PERD
DANS LES PREMIERS 50 KM
PUIS ATTITUDE DE BALLES
DOUM-DOUM C'EST LÀ LE
GRAND PROBLEME OÙ ELLE
POSERAIT A L'HEURE ACTU-
ELLE - AV DEPART ELLE EST
MONTÉE SUR UN DISPOSTIF LE
FORME CUBIQUE. DES BOUTE-
ILLES CONTENANT DU GAZ S'y
TROUVENT. - AU DEPART SUR-
GIT UNE FLAMME - LA FUSÉE
TOURNE SUR SON AXE SELON
UN MOUVEMENT EN SPIRILLE ET

STATION DESSAI et
POUR SOUS MAR INS AVIONS
PENEMUNDE
DE II
LAGER CARLSHAGEN
ZINOWITZ
WOUGASTE
FAHRE
CHEMIN DE FER
ROUTE
SWINEMÜNDE
USEDOM
PLAN CENERAL DE L'ILE
D'USEDOM

S'ENVOLE. - DISTANCE PARCOURVE SUREMENT 150 KM. PROBABLEMENT
250 KM. - L'USINE SUPERIEUSEMENT GARDÉE, 1 POSTE TOUS LE 10 M.
LE S.R. ALLEMAND CHERCHE DES ACENTS EVENTUELS

TRANSMIS PAR JEAN L'AVEUGLE

ACCUSEZ RECEPTION: BBC EMISSION POUR LE
GRAND-DUCHÉ.
"FIR DE BLANNE JANG 1-2-3-4 ARTHUR DE
JANG ASS DO"

FAMILLE MARTIN

PoWs, slave labourers and free partisans in the resistance movements provided invaluable information on V1 and V2 activities; this sketch, with detail, smuggled out of Peenemünde in June 1942. (Medmenham Collection)

twenty miles deep and stretching 300 miles from the border with Belgium down to the Cherbourg peninsula, with some ramps clearly pointing at Bristol. In addition, inputs from the PRU, PIU, CIU and Bletchley Park all suggested that the existing rail system from Germany through France was already in use to deliver missiles to the *Feldmulag* (field munitions depots), eight of which would be found by PR within the next six months.

Armia Krajowa (AK), the Polish Home Army, deserves special recognition for its intelligence exploits in East Germany and occupied Poland. Indeed, this group of courageous men and women provided 42 per cent of all the HUMINT gathered from Central and Eastern Europe, including information from inside the Nazi concentration camps. In particular, a special group within the AK had been tasked to continually update information on the rockets and flying bombs being developed at Peenemünde, one of its members being a disgruntled, anti-Nazi Austrian NCO in the *Wehmacht*, Roman Traeger, who was stationed on Usedom. In Poland itself, it had not taken long for the AK to confirm that flying bombs and the rockets were being tested at Blizna, and thereafter it provided valuable reports from the launch site and from along the V2s' flight path, as many of the rockets exploded in the air, shedding pieces along the route for the Resistance to collect and evaluate before the Germans arrived. Then, in May 1944, came their biggest coup of all, when a V2 crashed, with relatively little damage, close to the village of Sarnaki, on the River Bug, and was immersed below the surface of the water by the AK before the Germans could reach the area, and where it stayed until the partisans were able to disarm and dismantle it, ready for transport to Britain. On the night of 25/26 July, the pilot of a special, lightweight RAF Dakota made a covert, highly skilful landing and take-off at a disused German airfield near the site, to take the intelligence reports on the V2 prepared by the Polish aircraft designer Antoni Kocjan and significant parts of the rocket back to London. The package was also accompanied by Jerzy Chmielewski, who had many tales to tell as a witness to some of the firings in Poland. This very successful Operation WILDHORN (Operation MOST III, to the Poles), revealed valuable details on the construction of the weapon. The Poles also reported sightings of a complete V2, without its cover, in a railyard near Blizna and, most importantly, in June 1944, they discovered that liquid oxygen was part of the V2's fuel mix. Meanwhile, on 31 July in France, a dummy V2 and *Meillerwagen* were captured intact in a storage area at Haut Mesnil, Hauts-de Seine. All the rocket's secrets were now out.

That said, the Allies still needed to know when the V1 would become 'operational', and an offensive against Britain begin. By the second week of May 1944 they knew that twenty-two of twenty-nine flights from the modified sites trials at Zempin had been deemed successful, despite three being lost on radar, two falling short and two overshooting. On 11 May one crashed at Brostrap, in neutral Sweden, creating a flurry of activity which led to two specialist RAF officers, Squadron Leaders Burder and Wilkinson, flying immediately to the scene (by BOAC Mosquito) to bring back all the information they could. It transpired that this was the third V1 to fall into Swedish hands, none of which carried live warheads, but the two RAF officers were able to bring back useful details on the small, pilotless aircraft, with its crude, pressed steel cylindrical fuselage and 16-foot plywood wings. Other than the absence of ailerons, the flight controls were conventional, operated by three gyroscopes, one of which was aligned to the compass. There was no radio control, guidance being pre-set, and the simple pulse jet ran on low-grade aviation fuel.

While many in the Allied intelligence community were attempting to predict when, where, and how the V1 offensive would take place, others were monitoring the development of the V2 rocket. On 22 May 1944 a German sergeant, a chemistry graduate and specialist in rocketry, who had recently completed a course at Peenemünde, was captured in Italy, and during his interrogation at Trent Park, was able to provide reliable information on the A3, its construction, fuel (ethyl alcohol and liquid oxygen), launch equipment and design range. He also produced useable drawings of the *Bodenplatte* base plate and the *Meillerwagen* transporter/erector, from which the rocket could be launched, but he was unable to say much about the warhead, other than it was not chemical. Professor 'Bimbo' Norman, the Ultra specialist at Bletchley Park, and Lieutenant Colonel Matthew Prior of MI14 in London were also busy getting and giving information on the V2 tests in Poland and over the Baltic, and were now aware that a very large army formation, perhaps at corps strength, was being established for the V2 operations in France, using simple launch sites, consisting of little more than concrete bases, often with natural cover and AA protection nearby.

None of these pointers seemed to have had the immediate effect that might have been expected, with the RAF having accepted earlier predictions that a flying-bomb attack would not be likely for several weeks, and the Americans informed that there was no change in the threat to the Air Defence of Great Britain (ADGB). Perhaps the move of V1s from their storage depots, the sight of trainloads of missiles heading for the front, the intensive activity around the modified sites and the flurry of ominous signals detected by Bletchley failed to ring any bells, or these clear warnings did not reach or concern those responsible for the ADGB? Suffice it to say that the German missile men could hardly believe their luck, this apparent lack of reaction certainly helping the overture to their imminent offensive.

It was HUMINT which provided another wake-up call on 10 June 1944 when an agent in Belgium, believed to have been 'Junot', sent a message to the SIS that a train load of ninety-nine V1s, on thirty-three wagons, had just passed through Ghent, heading for Tourcoing, and that further train loads were expected. A day later PR showed that the modified site at Vignacourt had been completed and appeared to be ready to launch V1s.

Above and below: A V1 'ski site' under construction in Northern France in 1944, and a second, fully operational, with a flying bomb on its launch ramp. (Medmenham Collection)

Left: A typical V1 'modified site', well concealed in local surroundings - but visible from the air! (Medmenham Collection)

Below: Much remains to be seen at the standard ski site in the Bois des Huit Rues, Hazebrouck, Northern France, just enough being visible in 1944 for the PR and FR pilots to find and photograph. (Author)

All this, together with other snippets of intelligence, finally led London to the correct conclusion that a missile attack on England had to be expected on, or soon after, 12 June – and so it was. In the early hours of 13 June the first operational V1 was fired at London from the Saleux site in the Pas de Calais (Chapter Five). The campaign against the V1 may have been the responsibility of the operational staffs, the fighter and AA defences and passive defence forces, primarily, but intelligence inputs were still required, urgently, to help minimise the effects of this unique weapon, while the same staffs attempted to anticipate the impact of the now seemingly inevitable rocket offensive.

Home-grown HUMINT of another kind followed a few days after the initial landings in Normandy on 6 June 1944, when a specialist RAF officer went ashore tasked with finding a modified V1 launch site; this he did, ultimately to reveal all its secrets. In another piece of luck, an errant V2 rocket, fired from Peenemünde on 13 June, exploded over Bäckebo, scattering bits over the province of Småland, Sweden. The neutral Swedes investigated, collecting some useful data and hardware from the debris which, after satisfying lengthy protocols, found its way to England and into the hands of the technical intelligence experts at Farnborough. From their detailed examination, they were able to deduce that the rocket was powered by liquid oxygen, giving it a maximum warhead of two tonnes, and that liquefied gas provided essential cooling of the rocket's turbo-pump. Importantly, earlier intelligence that the missile's guidance system was controlled by radio, which could be jammed, was incorrect; the Bäckebo rocket was merely carrying radio equipment on trial for the *Wasserfall* missile (Chapter Nine).

Throughout the summer of 1944 Churchill assured the world that London was taking the V1 in its stride. Despite the destruction and number of casualties they had caused, the missiles had had little or no effect on production or the morale of the people, who continued to go about their daily routines as usual. Again to counter German propaganda, that 'London was a sea of flames', neutral observers were flown over the capital to show that this was far from the truth. In fact, there were few chances of hiding the truth, and behind the scenes there was disquiet and concern among the British politicians and military chiefs, that with the much vaunted Allied air superiority, Londoners were expecting to be better protected.

More useful information on the V2 came from the capture on D Day of *Obergefreiter* (lance corporal) Lauterjung, an intelligent, fervent anti-Nazi, who was interrogated by Denys Felkin at Trent Park on 20 June.

Lauterjung had been involved in the selection and construction of launch installations for the rockets in northern France, and was able to identify locations already under construction or being surveyed for that purpose. He pointed to a standard arrangement at Château Bernesq, with its three firing bases set along a stretch of road, and gave details of the launch facilities, together with the command and control arrangements. He also provided good information on a supply site he had seen in a quarry at Hautmesnil, complete with rail links between the tunnels and caverns in which the rockets would be stored before being loaded on to the *Meillerwagens* to transport and erect at their firing bases. On security and camouflage, he warned that some non-operational sites were still occupied, with French labourers present and visible to act as decoys for the Allied bombers. Another informant, *Obergefreiter* Klotz, was similarly willing to contribute to British intelligence on the France missile sites; captured at Saint-Lô, he was able to brief Felkin on a secure supply dump at la Meauffe, near Bayeux, that was ready and waiting for the rockets to arrive. They never did – the Allies got there first.

By mid-July 1944, with selected American officers now being given full access to British intelligence on the missiles, including Ultra, joint Anglo-American intelligence agencies were doing their utmost to locate all the V1 storage and launch facilities in northern France. They soon identified fifty-five launch sites, which appeared to be fully operational, and the records show that in one twenty-four-hour period in July, thirty-eight of these sites fired 316 V1s against London, twenty-five of which crashed after launch. The Allies were in no doubt now what they were up against, and in July a mixed force of RAF and USAAF bombers attacked 104 'Noball' targets. They were also fully aware that they might soon have to face the additional problem of a rocket offensive, and suspected (correctly) that the Germans, learning from their experience with the vulnerable V1 ski sites, were very likely to abandon the highly visible V2 'bunker' sites, in favour of tactical alternatives. In fact, on 18 July Adolf Hitler was reported to have ordered that the reinforced concrete V2 bunkers, and plans to launch the rockets from the ends of railway tunnels, be abandoned.

Also in June, signals picked up by Ultra indicated the movement of 'significant' but unidentified heavy equipment in East Germany and Poland, some mentioning a critical shortage of 'elephants'. Could they be the *Meillerwagens*, and connect with other information that V2s manufactured at Mittelwerk were now arriving for test firings at Peenemünde and Blizna? R.V. Jones thought that they were, and passed this on in a composite report to the Assistant Chief of the Air Staff (Intelligence) and the military chiefs on 9 July. By now, the V2 had been given the name 'Big Ben'.

The interrogation of German PoWs revealed that some were happily aware that the war was coming to an end, and they were quite eager to share what they knew about the V1s and V2s. One, *Leutnant* Krumbach, captured on 1 July, was able to outline the organisation of LXV Corps, in temporary residence at St-Germain-en-Laye and a subordinate unit, Höhere Artillerie Kommandeur *191* (*Harko 191*), roughly equivalent to an artillery division HQ, at Maisons-Laffitte, the units to which he had been posted. This was followed by another human source, a French agent who managed to smuggle out the latest information on missile production in the underground factory at Mittelwerk, drawing on details provided by prisoners at the Buchenwald and Dora concentration camps.

There was no lack of lateral thinking within the Allied intelligence community. Typically, there was a plan to evaluate the German missile performance over the Baltic, from tests at Peenemünde, by 'sowing' listening or tracking nodes, either on Swedish soil or by using Allied ships or submarines. Another idea called for airborne listening posts over Poland, provided by a rotation of specially-equipped, high-flying American P-38 Lightnings, while a similar SIGINT initiative, promoted by 'Bimbo' Norman, at Bletchley Park, suggested the use of the new American B-29 bomber, flying at heights generally above the effectiveness of the German air defences at the time. With the imminence of the Soviet army occupation of Blizna, neither of these plans were put into effect, but it was hoped that once the Russians had occupied the Heidelager range at Blizna, the Allies would be able to 'walk the ground', in search of those final elusive answers. To that end Churchill wrote personally to Stalin on 13 July 1944, alerting him to the new German missiles being tested there and seeking permission for an Anglo-American team of weapons experts to visit Blizna, as soon as it was occupied.

With Stalin's permission, all seemed set fair for the Allied mission to Blizna, Duncan Sandys succeeding in having his man, Colonel Terence R.B. Sanders of the Ministry of Supply, take the helm, together with another of his protégés, Geoffrey Gollin, the air intelligence officer Wilkinson, who had been involved with the Swedish V2, and a radio specialist Eric Ackermann. Moscow now realised that their allies had kept them in the dark about the new German weapons, so they mustered their own team of experts from NII-1, the Scientific Research Institute in Moscow, to pre-empt the British-led visit. The Russian Army occupied Blizna in early August 1944, and immediately began scouring Heidelager range for anything of technical interest. In fact they found little there that they could understand, and began to wonder if this was a ruse to get the British on to their front line – they would soon find out how wrong they were.

Meanwhile, Colonel Sanders and his Anglo/American research team had been mysteriously delayed in Tehran waiting first for visas and then for an aeroplane, only reaching Blizna on 3 September, where it was clear that the Russian search party had preceded them and taken away everything they thought of value. Even so, to the surprise of their Russian escorts, the well-informed British and Americans, having searched craters and even scrutinized papers found in the latrines, had filled several crates with useful artefacts and secured permission from the Russians to have them shipped to London. The initial report on the visit, from Sanders to London, spoke of warm relationships with the Russians at Blizna, and their belief that the pieces they had collected would be of great value when they arrived in Britain – but they spoke too soon. Fortuitously, they had carried out initial evaluations of their findings, because when the crates arrived in England, via a lengthy delay in Moscow, they were found to contain nothing more than rusty tank, truck and aircraft parts! That said, the Allies (less Russia?) now knew most of what they needed to know about the missiles, and in his second newsletter on 6 August, R.V. Jones, now deducing that, with the fuel weight known, the warhead would be in the 1- to 2-ton category. Bletchley concurred that the warhead was smaller than had been predicted.

Within the Intelligence armoury, counter-intelligence and deception were important weapons – and they were not neglected. Set up in 1941, the 'Twenty Committee' and the 'Double Cross' (XX), system, headed by John Masterman as part of MI5, were highly successful in 'turning' German agents captured in the UK to the Allied purpose, primarily to pass 'disinformation to their German controllers. Despite the public perception that the country abounded with these agents, it is believed that there were no more than twenty-five active in the UK at the end of 1940; with help from Bletchley Park's Enigma most had been picked up soon after insertion. Most were found to be far from the ruthless, highly-trained, well-skilled and motivated band expected, and some were ready and willing to turn against their original masters and spy for the British. To that end, those selected were nurtured in their new role at Latchmere House, Richmond, during which the Double Cross team learned much about the *Abwehr* (the German intelligence organisation).

As the V1 bombardment of London increased in the summer of 1944, the war of leaks, propaganda, deceptions and disinformation continued to grow on both sides of the Channel. Typically, the Germans used the double agent 'Garbo', the Spanish Republican refugee Juan Pujol, to let the British public know, by diverse means, that the V1 was only the first of the 'vengeance' weapons they could expect. Double Cross officers were equally determined that Garbo, who lived with his family in Hendon, North London, should be put to work for them on the rocket story and persuaded him to ask the *Abwehr*, through his handler in Madrid, whether there was any truth in the rumour circulating in London that an attack by 'an enormous explosive rocket' was imminent. If so, he would be prepared to remain in London to report on the 'fall of shot', but would move his family back to Spain. On 18 November 1944 he was told that there was no need for immediate concern, but on 16 December it was suggested that he send his family out of London. This turned out to be a somewhat premature warning – or was it deliberate disinformation? Duncan Sandys also mentions another prominent Double Cross agent, the Danish citizen Wulf Dietrich Christian Schmidt, alias 'Tate', who contributed much to British intelligence, and retired in England as Harry Wilkinson.

Another double agent, the Serbian Dusko Popov, codename 'Tricycle' (for his predilection to 'three-in-a-bed' sex), was tasked by the *Abwehr* to discover the purpose of two huge RAF runways at Woodbridge and Bentwaters, on the east coast in Suffolk, which they noted were heading at Berlin, and which they suspected might be designed as launch sites for British missiles similar to their own. In fact, these very long and wide runways were simply early safe havens for returning damaged Allied bombers, but the Twenty Committee seized the opportunity to nurture the German suspicions by building dummy installations on the twin airfields, supported by carefully staged leaks to suggest that Berlin could expect imminent threats from new weapons similar to those facing London. This XX plan then became more ambitious, hinting that the runways were there to launch 'super long-range rockets and radio-controlled aircraft carrying twenty tons of explosives all the way to the German capital'. Had these stories been believed, these airfields should have expected heavy air raids, but none were forthcoming, and both runways were used continually throughout the subsequent Cold War.

Given the abundance of raw information now available to the Allies, and the intelligence which flowed from it after detailed analysis and cross-checks, the threats were surely clear and countermeasures could be prescribed, yet there still remained tensions and fundamental disagreements between the parties involved, with consensus sometimes hard to come by as time was quickly running out. Typically, Lord Cherwell and the Home Secretary, Herbert Morrison, believed that they were still not being given full access to information available to Bletchley Park and R.V. Jones. Likewise, the Big Ben scientific sub-committee, which looked into the efficacy and likely ramifications of the V2, felt that they too were not getting the details they needed to prepare for and counter the new threat; was R.V. Jones being a little too zealous in protecting the sources? Once again an angry Churchill intervened, demanding that those involved, who had the right security clearances, be given all the information they needed to exercise their roles effectively.

In the early evening of 8 September 1944, two V2s, fired from Wassenaar, The Hague, in western Holland, landed in Greater London (Chapter Six), heralding another phase in Hitler's 'vengeance' campaign. In the days and months which followed, V1s and V2s rained down on England, mainly on Greater London, with monotonous regularity. The primary action now passed to the battle managers directly responsible for ADGB, which included, perforce, essential offensive action against the sources of these threats on the continent of Europe. Again, there could be no let-up in the intelligence work, now providing vital support for CROSSBOW, and these efforts will be covered in Chapter Eight.

Chapter 5

Open Fire!

On 1 December 1943 Colonel Max Wechtel's *Flak Regiment 155(W)* was absorbed into *LXV Armee Korps für Besonderen Verwendung* (65 Army Corps for Special Employment), commanded by *Generalleutnant* Heinemann, with Colonel Eugen Walter as his air force chief of staff. They were charged with the immediate preparation for the bombardment of England by the V1s and V2s, as soon as they became available. Although there was still much work to do on the V1 flying bomb, Wachtel was ordered to move his unit to northern France forthwith, and his advance units left Zinnowitz (Peenemünde) by train on 9 December, arriving at Merlemont, 8 kilometres south of Beauvais, on 13 December. The move, which would precede the weapons by some months, may have been a deliberate attempt to please Hitler, who was determined to repay London in kind for the damage the Allies were inflicting on the German cities. However, it did allow Wachtel's crews to become fully acquainted with their launch sites, technical, communications and re-supply systems, once they were up and running.

This was no easy task, given the almost continuous air attacks and no AA in place to ward them off, the regimental diary reporting that all their foreign labourers took flight whenever Allied aircraft approached. The devastation of the ski sites prompted the Luftwaffe to vacate them, other than those selected for deception and as decoys, which kept the Allies guessing, in favour of the easily camouflaged, randomly spaced, highly mobile modified sites, which 'melted' into the landscape, rendering them very much more difficult for the Allies to find and attack. This gave Watchtel's men some respite from air attacks and allowed them to consolidate their preparations for the opening offensive with a growing sense of confidence. The main delay now was blamed on a decision by the German leadership to give the V2 rocket priority over the V1 programme.

By now the whole German missile community had become obsessed with security, believing that many of their past misfortunes stemmed from intelligence passed to the Allies by PoWs, slave labourers and agents working on and around the weapons and their designated sites. Already, many foreign workers had been excluded from employment in sensitive areas and others were being heavily screened, all having to endure the harshest of penalties if there was any suspicion of transgression. This was grist to the mill for Heinrich Himmler, still bent on taking control of the new weapons. He had failed to do in 1943 and now argued that only his SS organisation could prevent damaging leaks reaching the Allies – but Hitler still vacillated. For added security, *Flak Regiment 155(W)* adopted the code name *Flakgruppe Creil,* while the four battalions were given the German names for 'Top Hat', 'Werewolf', 'Biscuit' and 'Sequin', the signals battalion becoming 'Vandal'. Max Wachtel, fearing that his arrival in France would give the game away, took security to a new level by removing himself temporarily to Paris, disguised with a beard and one arm, under the name '*Oberst* Martin Wolf', while his staff shed their uniforms and dressed as personnel of the German Construction Organisation Todt. These measures may not have deceived Allied intelligence but were said to have caused considerable confusion within the *Wehrmacht* itself.

Wachtel's preparations culminated in full-scale rehearsals for the opening offensive, with the launch crews, staffs, procedures and communications undergoing rigorous evaluation until their commanders were satisfied. The ultimate test came on the night of 1/2 March 1944 with the simulated launch of 960 V1s from sixty-four sites, some still incomplete, achieving excellent results and drawing many plaudits. The trials were also going well in Poland and along the Baltic coast where, by mid-May, twenty-nine launches from Zempin had resulted in twenty-two successful flights, albeit with one of the errant seven flying beyond its target area on 11 May to land in neutral Sweden (Chapter Four). Moreover, V1 and V2 production at Mittelwerk was now in full swing, deep underground and well protected from the prying eyes of Allied air reconnaissance and their bombers.

In the late spring of 1944 HQ LXV Army Corps moved to Paris, Hitler now decreeing that the bombardment of London should begin in mid-June. Reacting to the codeword *'Rumpelkammer'* (Junk Room), General Heinemann ordered the activation of all the operational V1 launch sites, the movement of the mobile launch ramps from Germany to the Channel coast and the missiles to their forward ammunition depots, these tasks being expected to take ten days. On 20 May Wachtel and his staff moved to their underground HQ at Saleux, near Amiens, and the launch crews to their sites, to await the codeword *Eis bär* (Polar Bear), thereupon to carry out final actions and open fire.

Having finally discarded the concept of launching their flying bombs from concrete bunkers and ski-sites, the Germans were able, subject to Allied air attacks, to move at will with their mobile equipment, and when the time came to remain ahead of the Allied invasion, which now seemed imminent; the great unknown was the timing. In fact, Operation OVERLORD, the landing of Allied forces in the Bay of the Seine, began on 6 June, a week before Wachtel's men were ready to launch their first flying bombs, but it did bring his force to the highest readiness state, with the movement of the regimental HQ farther east from the Château d'Auteuil to Château Merlemont, south-east of Beauvais, in the Oise region.

Despite full communications having yet to be established with all the sites, severe equipment shortages on the front line and woefully inadequate safety procedures, the V1 offensive began at 0400 hours on 13 June 1944, preceded by a long-range artillery bombardment against Folkestone and Maidstone, followed by the launch of a mere ten missiles. By the time *Oberst* Walter, at LXV Army Corps HQ, called the ceasefire at 0440 hours, only four of the missiles had reached England, five having crashed soon after launch and one simply disappearing. This was very far from the thunderous overture which had been demanded by the German leadership, and Wachtel was held responsible. He in turn blamed the 'dislocation of supply due to enemy action', but this was only one of the problems – and *Flak Regiment 155(W)* would have to do better.

Three days later, on the night of 15/16 June, it did better. *Oberst* Walter issued the fire order at 18.45, calling on all sites to open fire on London at 23.18 and continue firing salvos until 04.50. The first V1 left its ramp at 23.16 and by the time a ceasefire was ordered at 05.50, 243 flying bombs had been launched from fifty-five sites, one battery managing to fire successive bombs every thirty minutes. Of that total, nine exploded on ignition, destroying their launch ramps, forty-six crashed soon after launch and one simply ran wild over France, but 187 did reach England, with flight times to Greater London averaging twenty minutes. The weather was perfect for the raiders, with low cloud, rain and poor visibility making their acquisition and destruction very difficult. The German High Command and launch crews were jubilant and when *General* Heinemann and *Oberst* Walter were summoned to the Führer's presence at his forward HQ, underground at Margival, north-east of Soissons, Heinemann took the opportunity to request that some of his weapons be redirected to the English invasion ports of Southampton and Portsmouth. Hitler's response was predictable; he screamed, 'No! Hit London! Hit London!'

Left: A V1 launch team carries out final training before operational commitment. (Author, Courtesy HTM Peenemünde)

Below: The intended routes of V1 flying bombs were plotted from their respective launch sites, to intersect over central London. (Author's Collection)

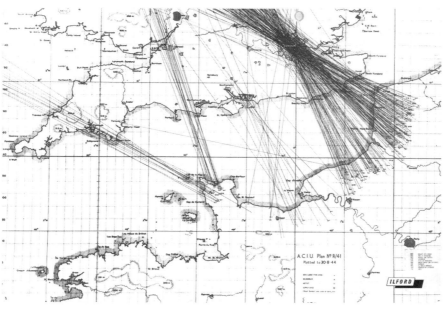

Spirits at LXV Army Corps HQ were high and the German public was elated by the comforting propaganda that the first of their *Vergeltungswaffen* had taken London by surprise, allegedly causing shock, confusion and panic, numerous deaths, injuries and damage to property, all purported to have been verified by German agents resident in London. This was a great exaggeration, designed to feed the growing German appetite for better news 'from the front'. The truth was that most, if not all, of these agents had been 'turned' and were now imparting information to their previous masters prepared by Britain's 'disinformation' specialists – operating under the name FORTITUDE. Their success was exemplified in Operation MINCEMEAT (and in the film of that name) which had laid a false trail on the Allies' invasion plans. Now, FORTITUDE came up with a plan which might minimise V1 damage to Central London. A highly-classified plot of the first impact points showed that most of the flying bombs were falling to the south-east of London, so double agent Garbo was ordered to pass a spurious plot to the *Abwehr* in Arras, showing that the majority were overshooting and suggested that the V1s' range be shortened, to bring them back to the centre, whereas in reality this would take the mean point of impact farther back to the south-east, into even less populated areas. In the event, the plan was put on hold, on the argument that the Germans probably had sufficient information from the British press, and perhaps from the tracking equipment aboard the V1s, to guess that this was an attempt to deceive, but it would be modified later and implemented later.

Intercepting radio communications and 'bugging' conversations in PoW camps, were not the sole prerogatives of the British (Chapter Four). On the other side of the Channel, *Oberst* Wachtel was delighted by the information he was hearing from airborne chatter between enthusiastic or frustrated RAF pilots tasked against the V1s en route to London. He heard, for instance, that his bombs were coasting into the UK at heights between 3,000 to 4,000 feet, at speeds of 340 mph as they accelerated to some 400 mph nearer the capital. Invaluably, he also learned that early acquisition by the fighter pilots was most likely at dusk, when the jet 'plume' was very visible and the interceptor could still judge his range to the target in the half light, that single V1s were relatively 'easy meat', whereas several arriving at once were bound to get through the defences, and he amended his tactics accordingly.

Wachtel's main concerns now were that the air attacks on V1 storage depots and transit routes, particularly those in the Oise valley, were severely effecting the resupply of missiles to the front, and that fewer of his V1s were reaching England owing to the increasingly effectiveness of the air defences.

Above and below: Outline maps charting the predictions of V1 landfalls and the actual impact points in the first 24 hours of the campaign.

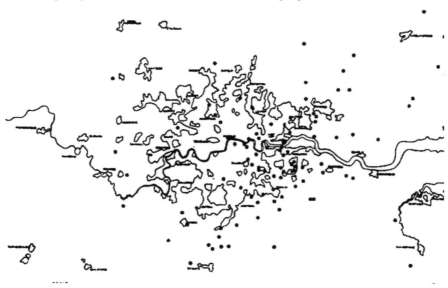

However, the overall success of the offensive, as seen by the Germans, resulted in authority for Wachtel to raise four more firing batteries and search for sixty-four new launch sites. This fact did not escape Bletchley Park which, on 17 July, picked up signals showing that a second regiment, *Flak Regiment 255(W)*, was to be formed at once, and that a third was mooted. There was no shortage of potential sites, the construction of which had become so refined that it could take as little as ten days to complete, in relative obscurity and invulnerability, while increased security discipline within Luftwaffe signals procedures was also making them hard to find.

The Germans may not have known exactly how many of their bombs were falling on critical areas of London, but by the end of July 1944 they were convinced that the capital was being devastated and the mood within *Flak Regiment 155(W)* HQ at Saleux was still upbeat, with its sub-units continuing to maintain the maximum possible continuous bombardment of London. Moreover, the number of V1s launched over the North Sea from modified Heinkel 111 bombers of Luftwaffe's *III/KG3* (No.3 Squadron of No.3 Wing), was increasing, giving the Allies the additional problem of defending a much wider range of additional flight paths to London. Also raising new concerns, Bletchley Park reported that trials on ground and air-launched V1s seemed to be going well in Poland and over the Baltic, possibly with a new, long-range variant of the missile. August also began well for *Flak Regiment 155(W)*, with thirty-eight operational sites firing 316 missiles on the night of 2/3 August, these approaching the UK in waves, between heavy cloud layers, again making life very difficult for the defenders – but only 107 of the bombs reached Greater London.

By mid-August the Allied forces were fast approaching the V1 launch sites in northern France, and some of Wachtel's units were already on the move north-east, the gunners preparing to re-role as infantry, while destroying anything of military value as they went. The Flak Group HQ was also on the move and, on 18 August, Colonel Walter and the main HQ of LXV Army Corps departed north into Belgium, while the launch sites continued to fire their missiles until the enemy was very close, before redeploying under cover of darkness in the hope of avoiding the attention of Allied air power sweeping ahead of the ground troops. On 1 September the last V1 was fired from French soil, but the flying bombs were not finished; *Flak Regiment 155(W)* had fled France successfully with much of its equipment and a number of bombs, and more were known to be in the pipeline; where would they go now, and what would be their targets? And of course the air-launched threat remained. With London temporarily out of reach, *Generalfeldmarschall* Model (C-in-C West), ordered Wachtel to find thirty-two suitable launch sites, some in the Eifel, on the Belgian/German border, others south of the Ruhr and east of the river Rhine, to be ready to bombard the Allied forces approaching the Mons-Brussels-Antwerp region.

Meanwhile, in the second half of September, the highly ambitious and hugely risky Allied airborne Operation MARKET, secured the river crossings at Eindhoven and Nijmegen, but crucially failed to take that over the Rhine at Arnhem. All of these crossings were vital to a rapid Allied ground advance into northern Holland and encirclement of the Ruhr (Operation GARDEN), while cutting off the German missile forces now mustering in strength at sites in western Holland – and perhaps finishing the war by Christmas. Had MARKET GARDEN succeeded, it is most likely that the German missile men would have been pushed north and east out of Holland, putting London out of range of their V1s and V2s – but this was not to be. The failure of MARKET GARDEN gave the Germans new hope, and Max Wachtel himself remained optimistic, believing propaganda claims that England would capitulate if the missile bombardment extended into middle and northern England. True, it would be some time before his units would be able to do so with their new, longer-range V1s, now known to be undergoing trials at Peenemünde, from ground sites in north Holland, but rockets were now falling, albeit sporadically throughout England, as were V1s delivered from Heinkel 111 bombers flying off the coast of Yorkshire against Manchester. In fact, only one V1 fell in the Manchester area, causing a number of deaths and badly injured, but this did presage another headache for the defenders.

Meanwhile, Wachtel was back in Germany, developing the thirty-two sites from which his V1s might help to delay the invading forces, two batteries deploying to the Eifel, primarily to contribute to an offensive against the all-important port city of Antwerp. Both sides were well aware that the port of Antwerp was going to be crucial to the Allied advance to the north and the east, so General von Zangen's Fifteenth Army was called on to defend the Scheldt Estuary, to the last man. While Antwerp fell to the Allies on 4 September, the Germans held out on South Beveland and Walcheren Island until 26 October and 9 November respectively, denying access to the port, and it was not until the end of November that the Royal Navy was able to clear the Scheldt Estuary of mines, and allow Allied shipping to bring in the much-needed supplies. The Germans had warned the residents of Antwerp that, if their town fell to the Allies, they would feel the full wrath of 3,000 Luftwaffe bombers, but severe shortages of fuel and aircraft, let alone Allied air superiority, rendered such 'retribution' a hollow threat. Instead, the Germans carried out a massive attack by V1s and V2s, fired from the north, the east and the south-east. With this flexibility, and the shorter range from launch sites to target, the Allies were, arguably, given more problems than they had had with the defence of London.

Overall, the air defence of Belgian cities was the responsibility of a British general, Major General A.M. Cameron, a reputable AA officer but with little experience against the V1, so the defence of Antwerp became a joint Anglo-American command, with the US Brigadier General Clare H. Armstrong effectively in charge. Armstrong's staff estimated that the Germans had the capacity to launch 105 V-1s and forty V-2s daily, against targets within the most important 12 square-mile area of Antwerp and, at that rate, given the inaccuracies of these weapons and the air defence forces at their disposal, they believed the war would be over before operations in the port could be seriously affected. They were wrong.

The Allied air defence assets were impressive, initially 11,500 men served within three AA brigades, two under American command, the third under the British, but as the campaign grew in intensity, the total number of men would increase to 22,000. The hardware consisted of 208 American 90mm guns and an initial British contribution of 128 × 3.7-inch guns, 188 × 37mm and 40mm guns, all of which were replaced by American weapons in November. The British also provided seventy-two searchlights. The guns were deployed in an arc spanning the south-east sector, well outside the city, in the hope that damaged V1s would not glide into the critical target area. Special measures were established, using time and space to co-ordinate fighter and AA operations, and to protect the many other Allied aircraft operating from local bases in the area from friendly AA. This was a particular problem for aircraft using the very busy major airfield at Hoogerheide (B79) north of Antwerp, which lay beneath one of the main missile streams, a problem only partially resolved by restricting flying there for specified periods. Another problem concerned the radars in use in this surrounding flat, wet terrain of the region, dotted with hundreds of small villages and windmills, which produced a great deal of ground clutter on the screens; optimum sites were, therefore, of paramount importance. While the SCR 584 radars in use were 'state of the art' and should have been able to distinguish between the V1s, with their small radar blip, steady course and height, and the larger Allied aircraft flying pre-planned, procedural flight profiles, mistakes were made. As for the guns, continuous use of the American 90mm M1 anti-aircraft gun for twenty-two of every twenty-four hours, with only two hours of maintenance, was taking its toll, and many of the guns needed barrel changes after firing 1,500 to 2,000 rounds, or the replacement of other crucial pieces of equipment. Failure to do so could seriously endanger the gun detachments. These and other factors led to many changes in air defence force deployments and tactics as the battle against the flying bombs progressed.

In these circumstances, given the V1s' speed and short flight time, there was little warning of the V1s approaching Antwerp, and this, coupled with the difficulties of co-ordinating AA and fighters in the crowded airspace, meant that interception rates were relatively low. So it was that much emphasis was placed on offensive action against the launch sites, but here again there were major difficulties. Despite the collective efforts of a wing of 2TAF fighters based at nearby Ursel, and twelve squadrons of Fighter Command Spitfires deployed daily from England, all carrying out continuous seek and strike missions, often dropping 500lb or 250lb bombs on areas thought to be harbouring or launching the missiles, success rates were again low. Attacks against the supply system and rail network often proved more profitable, but with German working parties carrying out rapid repairs at night, when darkness hampered fighter-bomber operations, they had only limited success. The night-fighter squadrons, amongst them the USAAF's 422 and 425 Squadrons, flying the radar-equipped P-61 Black Widow, had little difficulty identifying the flying bombs at night, but they found the small targets, flying at near their maximum speed, hard to destroy, and night interdiction against the railway network was again their preferred role. All that said, the various defenders of Antwerp deserve much credit. In the 175 days of the campaign, 4,248 V1s may have fallen in the vicinity of the city, with 211 getting through to the 'critical zone' and 150 reaching the crucial docks, but, working around the clock without adequate manning, they destroyed 2,183 V-1s, at a cost of thirty-two men killed and 289 wounded. They had done well. But then came the V-2s.

On 8 August 1944, with complete disregard for the crucial parts paid by Dornberger, Heinemann and Walter in overcoming all its problems and bringing the V1 to the front line, *Oberführer-SS* Hans Kammler replaced Walter Dornberger as Director of the V2 programme, taking full responsibility for its forthcoming operations. Ignominiously the three key players were relegated to the dissemination of the intelligence, storage and delivery of the rockets, final launch preparations and guard duties, but all now under Kammler's eagle eye and, by association, that of Heinrich Himmler himself. Kammler made his inexpert presence known at once, setting up *Gruppe Nord* (Group North) and *Gruppe Süd* (Group South), under a single *Division zur Vergeltung (*Revenge Division), with *Oberst* Thom as chief of staff. Headquarters for the division was at Nijmegen, on the German/Dutch border, and it was from there that Kammler ordered his 6,000 rocketmen, with their 1,500 vehicles, to prepare at once for an attack on London. LXV Army Corps had little to say in the matter.

London was not to be the first target for Hitler's final vengeance with the V2; that dubious honour went to Paris, well within the range of the

Lehr und Versuchsbatterie 444 (Demonstration and Experimental Battery 444), deployed near the Belgian town of St Vith, in the Ardennes. The offensive was scheduled to begin on 6 September 1944 – but all was not well. After being fuelled with eight tons of liquid oxygen and alcohol, the first rocket ignited successfully, only for its engine to cut out as it began to rise from its stand, leaving it to sink back harmlessly on its haunches. A second behaved in exactly the same way, the fault then found to be in defective accelerometers. Kammler was not amused. Following remedial action, the battery launched two rockets from the village of Petites Tailles, Ardennes, on 8 September. The first exploded in mid-air, but the second made military history that day, with the first successful flight by a ballistic missile in anger, to land in the south-east suburb of Paris, killing sixty Frenchmen and injuring thirty-six others.

Then it was London's turn, with two rockets fired on 8 September 1944, from a road intersection at Wassenaar, a suburb of The Hague, in Holland, by *Artillerie Abteilung 485* (Artillery Regiment 485). Despite heavy security, some Dutchmen witnessed the launch, after the support vehicles had moved away from the mobile launch pads, leaving only the armoured control vehicle on site. The two rockets lifted off cleanly in a cloud of smoke and flames at 1837 hours, and set heading for London, presaging another stage in Hitler's brutal revenge. The bombardment of England, primarily London, then continued apace, despite every effort by Allied air power to find and destroy the fleeting, highly mobile V1 and V2 targets, often at great risk to the friendly, supportive people within heavily populated areas in west Holland.

In mid-September, anticipating that the Allies might be successful in taking the crucial bridges over the river Rhine at Arnhem, in Operation MARKET GARDEN, thereby cutting off the two batteries of *Abteilung 485* in the area around The Hague, Kammler ordered them back to Germany, to be co-located with his HQ in Münster. At the same time, *Abteilung 444,* now similarly under threat at Walcheren, moved to a small wooded area at Rijsterbos, near Zwolle, in central Holland, and it was from there that the Germans sent their first V2 to East Anglia, at 20.00 on 25 September, to land harmlessly in the village of Hoxne, Suffolk.

Sensing that the timing might now be right, Hans Kammler made another bid to bring the Luftwaffe flying bombs under his command; he failed again, but took some comfort in the success with his rockets. In the last week of September, twenty-six V2s landed in Greater London, and eight elsewhere in the east of England, causing 235 casualties, with an unprecedented success rate of 76 per cent.

Blast-off. A V2 powering off from its *Meillerwagen* launch rig. (Medmenham Collection)

From October several major towns in Belgium came under attack from the V-weapons, but the primary targets on the Continent were Antwerp and Liege. The first V2 struck Antwerp on 7 October; by the end of the month 145 civilians and military personnel had been killed, with 223 injured. The city of Antwerp, full of military men and the paraphernalia of war, suffered grievously, soldiers and civilians working side-by-side in courageous rescue and recovery activities. Meanwhile, the essential unloading of supply ships in Antwerp harbour, which began in late November, went on continuously, albeit with periodic interruptions, the Americans being in charge on one side of the port, the British on the other. Within the first week of the port opening, the initial target of discharging 10,000 tons of mixed cargo per day had been exceeded, and in the first week of December this rate had climbed to 19,000 tons per day.

Liège, which had become a huge Allied supply centre, provided another lucrative target for Wachtel's flying bombs when the hard pressed Germans on the front line sought help to redress a dearth of heavy artillery. The city, with its several key rail nodes came under siege in mid-November, taking everyone there by surprise, and within the next ten days the residents, permanent and transient, suffered the alarming effects of 331 V1s. This was to be the beginning of a sustained offensive, which came in two phases. The first phase lasted until 30 November, after which there was a pause before the second phase began on 15 December, when Luftwaffe bombers and fighter-bombers joined the flying bombs in a continuous bombardment of the Liege railyards.

At the end of September 1944 the mood in London was again sombre; MARKET GARDEN had failed, leaving the way clear for the rocketeers to return to the west and north of Holland – within V2 range of England. The elusive *Batterie 444,* which had begun roaming around Friesland in the north, fired its first rocket into East Anglia on 1 October; it landed fifteen miles south-east of Norwich, close to the USAAF base of Hardwick, wounding four people and reminding the Americans that their air bases in that area were now on the front line. *Group Nord* fired its first rocket at London on 3 October, Wanstead, East London, being on the receiving end. On 12 October Hitler ordered *Batterie 444* to concentrate on London and the port of Antwerp, while the rocket units of *Group Nord* moved freely around The Hague, from one hideout to another, firing V2s at random from multiple sites. *Heeres-Lehr-und Versuchsbatterie 444* and *Herres Artillerie-Abteilung 485,* fired eighty-two V2s into London in November; 133 were scattered over south-east England in December and many more would follow in 1945.

The V1s and V2s were not the only new weapons of their sort to make their debut operationally in the latter stages of the war. By 12 December 1944 some 115 *Rheinbote* long-range rocket guns had rolled off the RMB production lines in Berlin Marienfelde; 222 more were promised in January 1945. By the first half of December, *Oberstleutnant* Alfred Troller's *Versuchskommando Artillerie Abteilung 709* was well trained on the weapon, had most of the necessary support equipment and had occupied a launch site at Nunspeet in central Holland. The battery was to have consisted of two weapon platoons, each having four fire units, but initially only one was deployed, together with its HQ staff, survey party, communications, security, maintenance, defence and transport sections; it was scheduled to begin firing its projectiles on 24 December.

Before then, however, the Allies were in for another rude shock and a major setback when, on 16 December, the Germans launched *Unternehmen WACHT AM RHEIN* (Operation WATCH ON THE RHINE) – which became known as the Battle of the Bulge (Chapter Ten).

Chapter 6

Homeland Defence

The defence of the United Kingdom in the final year of war depended on three distinct but interlinked components: offensive action, active defences and passive measures. Offensive action is often seen as the best means of defence, and in theory it could all but negate the need for the other options, but it had its limitations. In this scenario it would require the complete destruction of all aspects of the flying-bomb and stratospheric rocket research and development, trials and production. Unfortunately, this would be a wholly impractical proposition, given that a fully successful offensive against all these interdependent targets presupposes that they could all be located, that they would be vulnerable to contemporary weapons, and that the attacking force had a complete, day and night, all-weather capability to maintain a continuous campaign against them all. This being nigh impossible, offensive forces must be complemented by active and passive defences.

In the context of this work, the active defences required a radar, visual and audio warning network, fighter aircraft, anti-aircraft artillery and barrage balloons, all co-ordinated by a command and control structure, run by well-trained and rehearsed specialists, with back-up facilities, comprehensive communications and in-built redundancy. Sensible foresight in the 1930s had laid the foundations for these elements of an effective air defence of the UK, albeit with inadequate resources, especially in fighter aircraft and trained pilots, which necessitated a rushed programme to make up numbers. It is frequently claimed that the system which emerged, just in time, saved Britain from the might of the Luftwaffe in 1940 and, by extension, from a seaborne invasion by German forces, and there is no doubt that Britain's much enhanced active defences again did much to reduce the impact of the flying-bomb onslaught in 1944/45. Sadly, the same air defence system could provide no such protection against the supersonic, stratospheric V2 rockets; they had to be stopped at source by offensive action against the associated research and development centres, primarily Peenemünde, the logistic support facilities and launch sites, where they could be found (Chapter Eight). The ultimate solution could only be achieved by the invasion forces occupying all launch sites within the missile's range of the UK; no other action would be wholly successful, leaving the final component of defence, 'passive defence', to limit the casualties and expedite a return to some normality. In the background, contributing to all aspects of air defence, were the scientific and technical, civilian and military intelligence staffs, scrutinising air reconnaissance photographic evidence, together with objective and subjective inputs from myriad HUMINT sources, such as spies, agents in the field and PoWs, melded with SIGINT interpreted at Bletchley Park (Chapter Four). Homeland defence was a team effort.

Despite scepticism in some high-level quarters (vide Lord Cherwell) that neither the German army nor the Luftwaffe would be able to mount effective V1 or V2 campaigns against Britain before the time ran out for them, wiser heads prevailed, and plans for the defence of the UK were updated accordingly. On 2 January 1944, Air Marshal Sir Roderick Hill, Air Officer Commanding-in-Chief (AOC-in-C) Fighter Command and the Air Defence of Great Britain (ADGB) issued the first rudimentary plans for the defence of England against the flying bombs. These plans would be extensively modified in the light of events as they unfolded, but the fundamentals were as follows:

Early warning of incoming V1s would be provided by the ever-ready long-range radar systems lining the south-east coast, visual sightings from ships in the Channel and the Royal Observer Corps (ROC) over land, once the missiles crossed the coast. The codename for the V1 would be 'Diver'. Thus alerted, the comprehensive command and control network would pass relevant information to all the units in the sectors likely to be involved, and commit the defence forces as required. Radar-controlled fighters would operate well forward over the Channel, astride the V1s' expected approach lanes, seeking to destroy the flying bombs harmlessly over the water. Given the expected speed of the flying bombs (350-400 mph), the fastest fighters available had to be withdrawn from elsewhere in the UK and from assets designated to support the Allied forces as they advanced across Europe. Day and night, the interceptors would be guided to their targets by the fast developing UK radar system in the south-east, again assisted by visual reports on the tiny aircraft from the ROC.

With this help, target acquisition and identification by the fighter pilots should not have been difficult, given the V1's very visible jet plume within an inbound height band of 2,000 to 6,000 feet, unless the missile was in cloud. Catching and destroying them was another matter, as they accelerated to 400 mph in UK airspace, unless the older Spitfires, Mustangs and Thunderbolts, with which most of the fighter squadrons were still equipped, were in an optimum position, above and close behind a V1, when the pilot made visual contact, enabling them to convert any height advantage into speed; otherwise, they were just too slow. The latest Mustangs, the Griffon-engine Spitfire XIV and the new RAF Tempest V propeller-driven fighters, and certainly the Meteor jet just coming into service had the necessary speed to overtake, and they would be heavily committed against the flying bombs, but again at the expense of other roles. Initially, bringing down the doodlebugs would be a matter of trial and error.

The initial air defence matrix had the fighters on the front line, patrolling over the sea, free from any interference from the guns. On the coast there was a belt of 576 light anti-aircraft (LAA) guns (40mm weapons), with another 560 LAA equipments of the RAF Regiment. Forty miles north-west on the North Downs lay the main zone of medium and heavy AA, from East Grinstead to Gravesend, with the barrage balloons behind them as the last line of defence. With complicated rules of engagement, some reliance on visual identification between the V1s and the fighters and the risk of AA and fighters operating in the same airspace, conflict between the two seemed inevitable. General Pile, in overall command of British and American AA, and that of the RAF Regiment, knew that the heavy 3.7-inch British guns, currently operated from their well-prepared static bases, were not capable of the rapid re-deployment which might be necessary. Accordingly, he ordered hundreds of 'Pile Platforms', to be made out of 'a lattice-work of steel rails and sleepers and rails which, when filled with ballast, was as static as anybody could desire', thereby giving the units much greater mobility. A compact gun belt from Beachy Head to Dover was created, 5,000 yards deep and firing 10,000 yards out to sea. The move of the heavy guns began on 14 July and was complete three days later; the light guns were in place by the 19th. To assist the gunners, an array of searchlights illuminated the sky at night.

The numerous silver barrage balloons, ranged across Greater London, its environs and on the North Downs to the south, had sites hurriedly prepared for them by the Airfield Construction Branch. Balloon Command had its headquarters at Towerfields, two miles north of RAF Biggin Hill, and it was from there that all Diver operations were conducted. By mid-July 1,750 balloons were in place, in a 'half moon' stretching from Redhill to Chatham, thirty-one miles long and eleven miles deep, making a beautiful sight but bringing small comfort to the residents below, who might be on the receiving end of any missiles brought down upon them. Likewise, those on the ground manning the balloons also had to be ready to run for their lives if a V1 snagged their balloon cables and spun to earth among them. The balloons also presented a hazard to any unwary Allied pilot, especially in poor weather and at night, and more than one would come to grief as a result. For much of the V1 campaign the balloon units were manned by airmen, servicewomen being confined largely to the myriad support duties. This whole air defence matrix did not have long to wait before it was put to the test.

At about 04.00 on 13 June 1944 the ROC Centre at Maidstone, Kent, warned its forward observation posts that 'something was brewing in the Boulogne area' – and so it was. Next came a report from a Royal Navy motor torpedo boat in the Channel that an unknown object, a small aeroplane spewing flame, could be seen just to the north of Boulogne, heading for England at about 1,500 feet. Through his binoculars, Observer Edwin Woods, manning Observer Post (OP) Mike 3, in Kent, reported what he thought was a 'small fighter on fire', heading for London – but just outside his area of responsibility. Accordingly, he passed this information on to his colleagues, Observers Woodland and Wraight, at OP Mike 2, in a Martello tower at Dymchurch, who picked up the flying object at 04.08, noting red flames spurting from its rear end, and making a noise like 'a Ford Model T going up a hill'. The ROC had been warned what to expect, and Woodland reported his sighting according to the pre-briefed format. This alerted the ROC Control Room at Maidstone, and thus the whole of the air defence system in the south was brought to immediate readiness. Within minutes the Air Ministry in Whitehall also knew that the new campaign had begun and, at 04.13, the first of thousands of V1s to hit England began its death dive overhead Swanscombe, Kent, landing harmlessly in a field beside the Rochester-Dartford Road, leaving a three-feet-deep crater surrounded by the metal remains . Three others landed that morning (Chapter Seven), and while there was no official acknowledgement that new air weapons had arrived, Lord Cherwell was heard to proclaim, 'The mountain hath groaned, and brought forth a mouse'. But much worse was to come.

A second wave of V1s took to the air on the night of 15/16 June, 244 bombs being launched and 187 reaching Greater London. Hill's fighters were quick to get in on the act at dawn, the tell-tale 'flaming tail' helping Flight Lieutenant Musgrave and his observer, Flight Sergeant Somwell, in their Mosquito night-fighter of No.605 Squadron, down the first Doodlebug

Residents of Greater London spent many noisy nights inside corrugated iron 'Anderson' shelters – with some creature comforts. (Courtesy Lowewood Museum)

of the war. Given the need for speed, No.150 Wing, with its three squadrons of Tempest Vs, commanded by Wing Commander Roland 'Bee' Beamont, were deployed to RAF Newchurch on Romney Marsh, and it was Bee, with his wingman Sergeant Bob Cole who, an hour after Musgrave's success, shared the second victory of the day against a V1, Cole finally sending it to its grave in a field south of Maidstone. By the end of that first day of real action against the flying bombs, 150 Wing was credited with eight victories.

At 10.40 on that 16 June, AA guns in Folkestone, Sussex, scored their first success against the V1s, and the gunners manning the AA belt to the south east were elated by the number they believed they had hit that day, only to have many of their claims rejected on the grounds that the engines had merely cut out, as designed, when they reached their target area. Beamont was far from amused when a message from on high stated that the fighter pilots could not claim 'kills' against the V1s which could not evade them, Bee arguing that they faced grave danger when attempting to 'gun down' a target in which 1,800lb of Amatol explosive could blow up in their faces. Indeed, in the first six weeks of the campaign, eighteen of the attacking aircraft were either destroyed or badly damaged in this way, five pilots and a navigator being killed. Beaumont also took the opportunity to complain volubly that his fighter pilots were being shot at by over-zealous AA gunners. The gunners, from General Pile downwards, seemed unrepentant, blaming the pilots for flying into a gun defended area (GDA), all this resulting in an air of hostility between the two UK defenders, which would take more than simple co-ordination measures to heal the rift.

The increasing value of the AA defences could not be denied, not only for bringing down the missiles, but also in helping maintain the morale of those on the ground. Most welcomed the guns, putting up with the risks and the noise, but others became more strident in their complaints, this in some cases resulting in the batteries being moved elsewhere – to the detriment of others. Those in Sussex believed they were having more than their fair share of the flying bombs and the damage caused by the guns spewing hot, jagged shrapnel on those below. Vibration caused by heavy guns firing close to ancient and fragile houses also resulted in serious damage, eighty-one houses in Portslade, Brighton, said to have been damaged in this way, and many residents were known to have left their homes between Camber and Rye Harbour, which hosted the biggest concentration of AA in the country.

As the intensity of operations increased in the summer of 1944, so did the effectiveness of the guns, given improvements in the radar, a new proximity fuse code named 'Bonzo', and the continuous practice enjoyed by the gunners. The AA screen on the coast destroyed sixty-eight bombs on one day in August, while the Americans did even better with their 90mm guns and the fighter pilots were excelling themselves in the air. These achievements were raising the defenders' morale sky-high, but there was a price to pay for this seemingly unending activity, with both the gunners and fighter pilots becoming very tired. They pressed on, driven by inevitable rivalry between all those involved, with the gunners steadily forging ahead, if a little sore that they were not receiving the adulation bestowed on the heroes in the skies. The balloon barrage claimed its first V1 on 20 June 1944, fortunately at no cost to those on the ground.

The mood at the War Cabinet Meeting on 16 June was sombre; this was not like the 'pinprick' of three days earlier, and the portends for the future were grim; the public was being kept largely in the dark as to the nature and likely extent of the new threat, but the truth could not be kept from them for much longer. The military chiefs, who had been led to believe that a major V1 assault would not begin for a further couple of weeks, had been suddenly ordered to reinforce and redistribute their defensive assets as best they could, while competing with the imperatives of the invasion forces now on the other side of the Channel. So it was with the offensive forces involved indirectly in the air defence of the homeland, with General Eisenhower, the Supreme Commander of all Allied Forces in Europe, having to divert some of his resources to attack the V1 launch sites in northern France. Lord Cherwell, having now accepted that the flying bomb was a reality, commented that attacks on V1 supply dumps serving ski sites thought to have been abandoned was wholly nugatory, and would risk valuable aircraft against those serving as heavily protected decoys, but this advice may have fallen on deaf ears, because the sites were bombed anyway.

The Spitfire XIV squadrons of RAF West Malling were next to join the defenders and it was from there that an Australian pilot, Flying Officer Ken Collier, was credited with finding an arguably less dangerous way of bringing down a V1. On the evening of 23 June, Collier found his quarry at 2,500 feet but, having failed to arrest its deadly progress towards London before running out of ammunition, he flew alongside his target, wingtip to wingtip, and having checked he was not over a built-up area, he succeeded in tipping the tiny aircraft on its back, sending it spinning into open countryside. There was no question as to the veracity of this story, paint marks on his Spitfire's wing having been conclusive, and many other pilots attempted, with varying degrees of success, to emulate this courageous act. On 1 July the Spitfires were joined at West Malling by the Mustangs of No.316 (Polish) Squadron.

Despite their successes, both Air Marshal Hill and General Pile felt that their respective fighter and AA defences could do better, and the debate on the best, collective way to down the V1s raged on between their staffs, each inclined to criticise the other. It seemed blindingly obvious that the conflict between the two systems stemmed primarily from overlapping operating areas, and that they should each be given their own 'playground', leaving the balloons as a last resort. Eventually they agreed that all the AA available should be deployed along a coastal belt, with their now highly efficient guns using automated gunlaying radars and firing variable time-fused shells, maximising the value of Anglo-American microwave early warning equipment, with a clear field of view over the sea. Well ahead, towards the threat, the fighters would remain the first line of defence, with a second sector

As a tail-piece to this issue show a Tempest fighter i pursuit of a Flying Bomb the English countryside n every effort to shoot it dow open fields where it will the least harm.

An RAF Tempest chases a V1 heading for London at low level (top right). (Medmenham Collection)

allocated to them over land, between the gun belt and the balloons. A mixed gathering of senior officers and experienced specialists from the two British services unanimously approved the plan on 14 July 1944, but without air staff or political representation. Sensibly, the protagonists rushed the plan to the Crossbow Committee on the same day, where Duncan Sandys decreed that this was simply an operational matter, well within the remit of the two commanders. The Air Ministry did not see it that way and refused to accept any responsibility for the outcome, but in effect they had been presented with a *fait accompli*, and there can rarely have been a more rapid redeployment of such magnitude, in part owing to the mobility of the big guns and their Pile Platforms. It also seemed to have been completed without the Germans' noticing. Initially, the V1 'kill rate' under the new plan was poor, but dramatic improvements were on the way.

Squadron Leader Bohdan Arct, officer commanding the Polish fighter squadron, had a particular hatred for the dreaded doodlebugs, imagining that their hideous cackling pulse-jet engine sounded like the laughter of wicked witches, airborne on their broomsticks, simply laughing at their intended victims. He was also contemptuous of the AA gunners, who did not seem to be able to distinguish between the very different silhouettes of the V1s and his Mustangs, too many of the latter suffering damage as

A British 3.7-inch anti-aircraft gun, on a mobile 'Pile Platform' in Southwold, the East Coast, in 1944. (Author's Local Collection)

a consequence. The pent-up fury of the Polish pilots, bent on revenge against the Germans for the atrocities they had committed on their beloved country, served them well in the air and, by the end of July, they had downed fifty V1s, before moving from West Malling to Friston, on the coast near Eastbourne, to carry on the fight from there. By the end of the campaign, No.316 Squadron had been credited with 300 victories against the V1s.

On 26 July 1944 Herbert Morrison , the Minister for Home Security, commissioned a review into the current state of the integrated defences, and how they might adapt to a combination of flying-bomb and rocket attacks. His 'experts' suggested that each rocket might result in thirty deaths, with many more injured, thus creating a degree of panic and a rush to escape from the capital (some 230,000 had left already), leading to serious political, social and domestic consequences, and he took these concerns to the War Cabinet. True to form, Lord Cherwell felt that such concern was precipitous, believing now that the rocket's warhead was likely to be much less than first thought, and that its guidance system might react to electronic countermeasures.

Morrison would prove to be right on the first premise but wrong on the second; the V1 attacks were now continuous, causing frustrations and perpetual loss of a sleep, in addition to the casualties and destruction, all combining to encourage more people to leave London. Mothers with children under the age of five were departing in large numbers and the railway stations were crowded with 'harassed, irritable and thoroughly uncivil crowds'. On 29 July twenty people had to be treated in hospital after being crushed in a rush at Paddington Station, prompting the Home Office to lay plans for a mass evacuation, should this be necessary in the event of an additional rocket attack.

Meanwhile, the two Tempest V squadrons of 150 Wing were excelling themselves, flying some fifty sorties a day from Newchurch and, by 23 August, they had destroyed 632 doodlebugs, 'Bee' Beamont himself amassing a score of thirty. Another 'ace', Squadron Leader Joe Berry, is thought to have held the record for destroying V1s in the air at night, bringing down seven on the night of 23 August alone. These night operations were particularly hazardous, exemplified by the loss of a promising literary figure, 20-year-old Flight Lieutenant James Farrar, who perished when his Mosquito was believed to have collided with its quarry.

The Meteor jets of 616 Squadron joined the anti-Diver operations for the first time in August, and on 4 August, Flying Officer Dixie Dean had the distinction of being the first jet pilot to bring down a V1. With a top speed of 485 mph, the Meteor was 65 mph faster than the Tempest, and 616 Squadron was soon scoring well. While the majority of the civilians on the ground had nothing but praise for the pilots involved, human nature explained some of the criticism of those who brought their targets down on the homes of victims below. Some towns escaped very lightly, Tunbridge Wells being one, escaping all but six of some 2,000 V1s which passed overhead on the way to London.

Privy to the deliberations on the potential rocket threat to England, those responsible for passive defence measures in the United Kingdom were now becoming increasingly concerned about the high probability of an excessive burden on the hard pressed civil defence organisation, particularly in London and south-east England. Given that offensive action and active defences could never prevent some, if not many, V1s and V2s reaching their target areas, passive measures would have to pick up the pieces, restore some degree of normal life and allow contributions to the war effort to continue. That was the purpose of the Air Raid Precautions (ARP) Committee, which met first in 1924, primarily to establish the principles on which a civil defence organisation could be based, and on which local councils could develop their own contingency plans. The government became more involved in the mid-1930s, creating an ARP department in the Home Office to provide additional guidance and instructions, a role formalised in 1938 with legislation as a resurgent Germany again threatened peace. Four basic components came under the umbrella of the ARP: the Auxiliary Fire Service (AFS), the Light and Heavy Rescue Services, the Decontamination Services (given the use of poison gas in the First World War) and the Air Raid Wardens – of whom there were more than a million 'front-line troops'. These services were organised within twelve Civil Defence Regions, sub-divided into groups, each to preside over a number of districts at the local working level. It was at that level that every attempt was made to co-ordinate all ARP actions and assist the many small groups of wardens operating in their assigned sectors, sometimes perforce without adequate communications, specialist forces or support equipment – simply relying on their own initiatives.

During the Blitz of 1940/41, the work of the fire and rescue services had been made more difficult by the continuing bombing, and the blackout necessary to deny the German bomber crews help in finding their targets; even lighted cigarettes were believed to give enemy pilots some clues, and streets would ring to cries of 'Put that light out!' Such extremes might not have been so important as the V1s rained down in 1944 but street lamps remained off and vehicles continued to have their lights shrouded, sometimes making vehicular movement very difficult, as attempts were made to prevent German reconnaissance aircraft assessing the damage caused by the flying bombs. Such would also be the case, but even more worrying, in the event of a V2 offensive.

The wardens' invaluable work is worthy of comment, and the author, sometimes acting as runner at his father's ARP post in Goffs Lane, Cheshunt, can do so from experience. The often very small, hastily-built brick shelters, some with concrete roofs to offer some protection from the bomb, could, at a pinch, accommodate four people, albeit with only two bunk beds among a mass of defence material. There were assorted protective garments, including gas capes and masks, tin helmets, a GPO and field telephone, first aid and decontamination kits, fire extinguishers, buckets of water and sand, long-handled shovels to remove incendiary bombs, lamps and torches, a radio, hand-held warning klaxons and maroons (large but largely harmless fireworks), and ear plugs. The walls were covered with local maps, myriad instructions on the most likely exigencies, and posters reminding everyone to 'Carry Gas Masks', 'Dig For Victory', 'Beat the Squander Bug', 'Switch that Light Off!', warnings that 'Careless Talk Costs Lives' urging everyone to 'Buy War Bonds' and to 'Keep Calm and Carry On'. The tasks the wardens might face, often as 'first responders' at a scene of devastation and misery, were too numerous to recall, suffice it to say that no two incidents were the same, some involving fire, collapsed buildings and unexploded bombs, casualties dead and buried under debris, broken gas and water mains, and no immediate help to hand. It went without saying that Air Raid Wardens had to be ready for anything, and for that reason realistic training began in earnest in 1939.

That, however, was easier said than done. Much of what follows is attributed to Edward (Ted) Carter, Chief Warden in the Waltham Holy Cross Urban District (in the author's area), just north of London, throughout the war. Ted's diaries underline the difficulties of replicating bomb penetration, blast and fragmentation damage, in perfectly serviceable, built-up areas. Casualties could be made very lifelike, but craters, burst water and gas mains, and the disruption they might cause, had to be simulated by those who staged the exercises. There were some splendid examples of individual initiatives, enthusiasm and determination, improvisation and make-do-and mend, although initially some very willing volunteers had difficulty getting used to the twenty-four-hour clock, and this resulted in 'some strangely wonderful timing', with emergency services arriving before a (paper) bomb had dropped. Communication breakdowns were easy to organise, as were outbreaks of fire, although these were inclined to get out of hand, given the use of readily available inflammable materials and training adjuncts. Ted Carter remembers a particular smoke-producing candle giving off such billowing clouds of sulphurous smoke as to induce hacking coughs among the wardens, casualties and spectators, which brought more than one exercise to an early end. On another occasion, those staging a fire were delighted with their efforts involving paraffin-soaked straw, smoke candles and practice incendiary bombs in a derelict cottage – until they realised that one of their number was still inside. Fortunately, this rather frightened man was small enough to be able to dive through an upstairs window, onto a bed of rubbish below, but he was not in a very good mood! Enthusiasm could be a mixed blessing. In the same area, over keen handlers of a newly acquired stirrup pump, demonstrating how to tackle a (non-existent) fire, filled the Upshire Village Hall with water – much to the dismay of those in charge. Their audience of 'first aiders' were so enthralled by this spectacle that they forgot all about their 'fatal and near-fatal casualties' nearby, who remained unreported and unattended to, eventually getting up and walking away. With so many 'casualties' unimpressed by their survival prospects, volunteers became increasingly hard to find. On another occasion, a volunteer unused to driving in the blackout with shrouded headlights on the minor roads in Epping Forest, had to ask the mock casualties languishing in his makeshift ambulance trailer to dismount and help him manhandle their vehicles back on to the correct road. Surprise exercises, by design, caught many off guard, such as one which began with several explosions and a fire at a derelict house in Sewardstone Street. The local wardens, quickly on the scene, wondered if they faced 'the real thing' when they were greeted with all too realistic 'blood-chilling screams' and actors who had made the most of their injuries, but they soon had the situation under control. Generally, no-notice incidents were unpopular, not solely because they would catch out the unprepared, but because they could bring normal life and important war work to a temporary halt. All that said, Ted Carter rightly claimed that, however imperfect their ARP exercises might have been, they taught many valuable lessons, which helped improve their reaction to live situations when they occurred. Some surprise tests might have been considered a little unfair, when there was no air raid alarm or raid in progress at the time, but that was also good practice for when the V2 rockets arrived without warning. Indeed, all these rehearsals, together with the live events staged by the Luftwaffe's bombers, in bringing all the military services and emergency services together in a joint reaction to diverse incidents, would serve the country well when it came to the combined onslaught by flying bombs and rockets. In the end, the damage and casualties inflicted by the V1s and V2s around the author's home were relatively light, compared with that in other areas of Greater London, but stories of them and others in the next chapter serve to illustrate the splendid, often courageous, work of the wardens and the ARP services in general.

With the Allies yet to break out of Normandy, and the imminent threat of another 'blitz' on London, more of the key players in the capital were beginning to side with Churchill on the possible need to at least threaten Germany with a major gas attack, Allied preparations for which were proceeding. Fortunately, in late July, the Allied forces began to make better progress on the ground, and again, a decision on the gas question was deferred. However, the rocket problem would not go away and Home Secretary Morrison raised the issue of evacuation again at the Rocket Consequences Meeting on 3 August, suggesting that the more vulnerable residents should leave the capital as soon as possible. Minister of Labour Ernest Bevin countered with his concern that this might cause panic with the inevitable loss of a large part of his essential labour force. In the event, it was decided that the Londoners should 'stay put', urged to take every reasonable precaution to protect themselves, while the authorities dusted off their evacuation plans – just in case.

From the second day of September an uneasy peace descended over London and it soon became clear that the last doodlebug had been fired from northern France. The euphoria was palpable; offensive operations against known V1 sites in France would all but cease, as would anti-Diver air operations in the south-east approaches. It was even suggested that the Crossbow Committee and the Rocket Consequences Committee could be wound up, but wise voices cautioned that, while known V2 sites in France might also soon be occupied, the rocket's greater range would bring them within reach of London from west Holland. Incredibly, in that first week of September, press releases prepared by Duncan Sandys and others said, in effect, that the country was no longer threatened by multiple flying bombs, with only a few likely to be air-launched, sporadically, from German bombers over the North Sea, and there was no mention of a longer range version of the V1 or of a rocket threat.

Churchill and others in the political and military establishment were far less sanguine; to where, they asked, had *Flakregiment 155* (W*)* fled, with most of its equipment and an unknown quantity of 'ready for use' V1s? Moreover, they felt sure that a new and terrifying phase of the war was about to begin, one in which there would be no warning of the incoming V2 rockets once they had launched successfully, and against which there would be no credible defence. True, some press releases were more cautionary, thereby confusing the general public, but the sceptics did not have to wait long for proof of their fears when the first V2 landed in Chiswick, West London, on 8 September 1944.

Strangely, the government thought it might be able to mislead the public into thinking that the sudden explosions occurring in and around Greater London could be attributed to exploding gas mains and, with no evidence of official concern, suggestion of evacuation, activation of the big underground shelters or attempts to deter evacuees from returning to London, some war-weary Londoners chose to believe this unlikely story. Perhaps the British government was hoping that Operation MARKET GARDEN would succeed, thus isolating the rocket units in west Holland and bringing the V2 offensive to an early close? Meanwhile, the German people were applauding the growing success of their new weapons, and it was German propaganda which forced the British government to come clean, disabusing the British public of the 'gas main' farce and announcing that a new weapon was now bombarding London. Although in the first two months only 1.6 people were killed and seven injured with each rocket which landed in England, this was small comfort to those directly affected.

The active defences in the UK, which had had such success against the flying bombs, were now at a loss to know how to deal with the supersonic, stratospheric rocket which could not, realistically, be intercepted in flight. Perhaps in desperation, General Pile suggested an imaginative scheme in which, on receipt of a rocket launch in Holland, his guns on the east coast firing airbursts, with each shell dispensing some 300 bullets into the path of the rocket as it returned to earth. However, the eminent pioneer of radar technology, Sir Robert Watson-Watt, felt that the chances of this bringing a V2 down was about a thousand to one, and nothing came of the idea, although Pile's independent scientific team had calculated that between 3 and 10 per cent of V2s could be destroyed in flight. The defenders soon concluded that the only means of reducing this new threat was to find and destroy the missiles before launch, together with their tactical support equipment, supply depots, means of transport and the production units. This was clearly a very big and difficult job, and it was one for the Allied offensive air assets, specifically the RAF and USAAF tactical air forces and the fighter-bombers from Fighter Command (See Chapter Eight: Code Name CROSSBOW). The ultimate solution was, of course, for the Allies to occupy all the sites associated with the rockets – but that was going to take time.

Understandably, given the nature of this unprecedented weapon, the V2 became a hot topic among the potential victims in the East of England, giving rise to many implausible but also perhaps a few true tales. Some claimed to have glimpsed the rocket micro-seconds before impact, they having been alerted to its impending arrival by the strange antics of their pets, while others on ships at sea and on the far-off coast of England, were said to have seen rockets, if only fleetingly, moments after their launch from sites in the west of Holland. More plausible were reports of the strange effects of the blast spreading from the rockets as they exploded on impact, of soot being sucked out of all the chimneys in a street by the vacuum created, patterns made by clouds of dust and glass 'shivering' like flowing water.

General Eisenhower now decreed that all Crossbow intelligence was to be passed to his HQ, and approved a change in the air defence command and control arrangements which would take effect during the second week of October. These included the disbandment of ADGB, Air Marshal Sir Roderick Hill reverting to his old role of AOC-in-C Fighter Command with additional responsibilities covering offensive operations against the V2 sites and all means of their support shared with the commander of the RAF's Second Tactical Air Force (2TAF), Air Marshal Sir Arthur Coningham. Initially, essential co-ordination of these responsibilities, and the task of downing the German Heinkels carrying V1s to England, proved unsatisfactory, so it was decided that Fighter Command would look for and attack any targets which threatened London in the west of the operating area, while 2TAF dealt with such matters farther east into Europe (Chapter Eight). In their air-to-ground operations, both organisations would be heavily committed to armed reconnaissance, or 'seek and strike' missions.

As the winter of 1944 approached an air of gloom persisted over London, and in particular among those in the establishment who were responsible for its defence against the indefensible rockets. The morning of 25 November was particularly bad, with very heavy damage caused by a V2 in Holborn, and another in New Cross. There was a feeling of helplessness everywhere; Bletchley Park was unusually quiet, although a little later it detected signals which outlined the organisation of the rocket forces within the *Division zur Vergeltung (AKzV)* (Division for Retaliation) with Group North at Kleve, and Group South at Euskirchen, both close to Germany's western border. Crucially, there was no way of finding the precise locations of their respective firing sites, reports from agents and from other sources arriving too late for offensive action to be taken before the missiles were launched and the units moved on to new sites. So it was that London and its environs continued to be raided night and day. However, the next trend was more favourable, the number of rockets fired per day dropping from eight to four in mid-December, this being attributed to more intensive patrols of the suspect launch areas by Allied fighter-bombers and the fact that the Germans were now having to re-supply and operate their firing units by night only, with all the difficulties that implied.

The stoic Londoners were listening to advice and doing all they could to protect themselves, many shunning crowded places, hurrying back from the capital to their homes in the outskirts and staying at home in the evenings. Outwardly, they continued to put on a brave face; they were all in it together, rich and poor alike against a common foe, but there was no denying that many of them were now showing signs of war weariness, looking tired, shabby and unkempt. To them, too, it was particularly depressing to know that there was no effective defence against the rockets, as German propaganda claimed that the 'centre of London was in ruins', and predicted that 'in another month there would be nothing left of the capital'.

The new year brought with it a renewed threat of V1s, those of Wachtel's units which escaped north into the Netherlands having been ordered to prepare for fresh attacks on London from sites in Holland as soon as possible. So it was that on 3 March 1944 thirteen of Germany's new lightweight, long-range V1s were launched from there, heading for London, but for reasons unknown only two crossed the coast and only one reached the London area, landing on Bermondsey. At that stage it was not known from where precisely they had been launched, but signals decoded at Bletchley Park in January confirmed reports from agents on the ground in west Holland that sites were being prepared for V1s there, and the first of these were found by RAF reconnaissance aircraft on 7 March, one at Ypenburg airfield, east of The Hague, the second at a soap factory at Vlaardingen, near Rotterdam, triggering immediate attacks against them.

Many more guns were now being moved to the east coast, from the Isle of Sheppey north to Orford Ness, while AOC-in-C Fighter Command ordered three squadrons of the higher-performance Mustangs to patrol over the sea, forward of the guns, and another three, together with the new Meteor squadrons, to do likewise over the land behind the guns, up to the balloon sector. Two Mosquito and Tempest squadrons provided the night guard. At the same time Fighter Command and 2TAF fighter-bombers continued their 'seek and destroy' missions against the elusive rocket sites and their logistic support. Bombing the huge, and sole remaining V1 and V2 production site at Middelwerk was considered again, but rejected on the grounds that even the British 12,000lb Tallboy bomb would neither penetrate the work caverns deep underground nor guarantee that the seismic effects would have the desired results. The USAAF thought of attacking the tunnel entrances, but this would demand very precise bombing and delay production only marginally. In January 1945 there were more demands for a concerted bombing campaign against the missile launch areas around The Hague using heavy bombers, but again these were rejected by the defence chiefs, given the inherent bombing inaccuracies of the heavies and the great risk to Dutch residents. However, in a desperate attempt to reduce the impact which the rockets were having on London, they did agree to precision attacks on carefully chosen targets around The Hague, by the medium bombers of 2TAF, a decision they might come to regret (Chapter Eight).

The public had the right to be concerned; despite every effort to find and destroy the V2 units and installations on the continent, 228 rockets reached England in January, 233 in February and 227 in March, but at 11.15 on 27 March 1945, the last V2 struck Orpington, Kent, with only one fatal casualty. A day later Britain's battle with the V1 doodlebugs also came to an end, with the penultimate missile coming down at Sittingbourne, Kent, and the final one brought down by the guns off Orford Ness. The rocket units would fire no more, but the flying bombs would continue to target Antwerp for the next three days. The active air defences of Great

Some Air Raid Wardens of the Urban District of Waltham Holy Cross, December 1941

Some of the Air Raid Wardens of Waltham Holy Cross, in December 1941. (Courtesy Janet Grove)

Edward (Ted) Carter, Chief Warden for Waltham Holy Cross, keeping an eye on an unexploded 1000kg German bomb. (Courtesy Janet Grove)

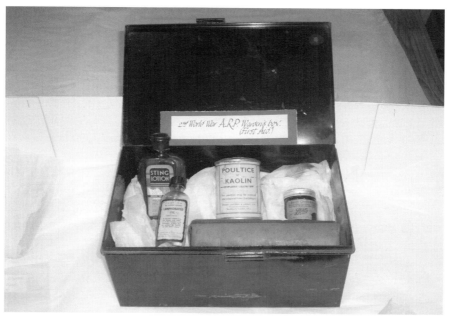

All ARP posts were equipped with very basic safety equipment, including these first aid kits. (Courtesy Lowewood Museum)

On 20 September 1944 Waltham Holy Cross Wardens set up this Incident Post, by the Green Man Public House, Waltham Abbey, to deal with the effects of a V1 which landed close by in Larsen's Recreation Ground. (Courtesy Janet Grove)

Britain, beginning with the comprehensive warning network, the efficient command and control system, fighter aircraft, AA and balloon units, had served their country well against the V1s, while the offensive assets did what they could against both V1 and V2 weapons sites on the continent, and the emergency services, professional and voluntary, excelled in their rescue and recovery work.

So it was that, from April 1945, all the offensive and defence air assets, which had worked so hard together to minimise the effects of Hitler's *Vergeltungswaffen,* became available to support the invasion forces on the continent, or to deploy to the Far East to take part in operations against Japan. On the home front, the passive defences and, in particular, the ARP were unlikely to be required at their present levels and preparations began at once to stand down most of the wartime volunteers. They and everyone in the peace-loving world celebrated Victory in Europe Day (VE Day) on 8 May, with great gusto while two powerful searchlights, from somewhere north of the author's home, made a gigantic V in the sky above. Ted Carter and the Waltham Holy Cross ARP paraded for the last time on 13 May 1945, the sirens had stopped their wailing and the nights were now left to the nightingales.

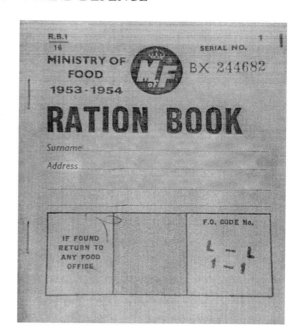

Right: Strict food rationing continued throughout the war and to a lesser extent until 1954. (Courtesy Lowewood Museum)

Below: ARP wardens wore their badge with pride. (Courtesy Lowewood Museum)

At the end of the war His Majesty King George VI, the Queen and the then Princess Elizabeth paid proper tribute to the men and women of Britain's Civil Defence. (Courtesy Janet Grove)

Chapter 7

Too Close for Comfort

What was life like for those, particularly in Greater London, who lived under a rain of flying bombs and rockets? Starting slowly in June 1944, the V1 offensive continued with increasing ferocity, day and night, until all the launch sites in the Pas de Calais were occupied by the invasion forces in September. There was then a long pause as Colonel Wachtel's ground-based units moved north to resume the campaign in 1945, with modified, longer-range V1s able to reach England from new sites in northern Holland, the last landing in Britain in March 1945. Meanwhile, the bombardment had continued, albeit sporadically with the V1s launched over the North Sea from Heinkel 111 bombers (Chapter Five).

The first four V1s hit England in the greying dawn of 13 June 1944, some early risers around Swanscombe, Kent, being the first to hear that soon to be familiar pulsating sound of its engine, as they watched the yellow fire emitting from its jet-pipe die and the bomb dive to the ground, harmlessly in this case, in a field on the A2 Rochester to London road. The time was 04.13. This was followed by a second, which hit Mizbrook's Farm, Cuckfield, Sussex, at 04.20, badly damaging some greenhouses and killing a few chickens. A third, by far the most serious that morning, struck a railway bridge on Grove Road, Bethnal Green, East London, at 04.25, killing six, injuring thirty and rendering 200 homeless amid extensive damage. A fourth came down at Platt, near Sevenoaks, Kent, at 05.06, without causing any casualties or damage. So ended the first day of a new 'blitz' on London.

In the first three days of the V1 campaign eighteen people were killed, 166 suffered serious injuries and eighty-three were slightly hurt, but much worse was to follow at the weekend. This began with twenty-four deaths in Battersea, on Saturday, 17 June, after which Westminster suffered from three V1 strikes during the morning of 18 June, the first on Hungerford Bridge, and a second on Carey Mansions, Rutherford Street, which killed ten and injured fifty in a fire which raged for seven hours. Then came the third, greater tragedy when, at 11.20, a V1 hit the Guards Chapel, Wellington

Barracks on Birdcage Walk, during the Sunday morning service, many notables being among the sixty-three servicemen and fifty-eight civilians killed, together with sixty-eight seriously injured. One worshipper, who suffered life-changing injuries, remembered the sinister sound of a V1 increasing as it approached, almost drowning the band, the renowned choir and collective voices singing the Te Deum, until its engine faltered and stopped almost overhead, leaving an eerie silence before a mighty explosion rendered the beautiful chapel to a hideous heap of rubble. This was the 500th V1 to be launched against London.

This being on the doorstep of the London establishment and ultimate authority, the flying-bomb threat was brought into even sharper focus; if this was Lord Cherwell's 'mouse', it was a mouse that roared – and the defenders of the homeland knew they must react accordingly. The civilian communities were already getting very worried, some taking shelter in the twenty-two miles of Chislehurst caves, south of London, while many schoolchildren were being kept at home and plans were advanced for another evacuation of London. While the visible effects of the defending AA and fighters was good for morale, the AA was deemed to be a mixed blessing, with many of the V1s they hit failing to explode and simply falling on those below, while at the same time the guns showered the area with unexploded shells and hot, jagged fragments, in a continuing crescendo of noise which caused sleepless nights and considerable irritation. The Government was now all too well aware that it must pay more attention to the morale of the tired inhabitants of London.

The War Cabinet Civil Defence Committee met on the next day, Monday 19 June, to be greeted with the news that, so far, 674 flying bombs had crossed the coast into England, of which seventy-six had been brought down by fighters and 101 by AA; 499 Londoners had been killed and 2,105 seriously injured, while the damage to property had been extensive. One of the War Cabinet's first actions was to resurrect the prematurely disbanded Crossbow Committee, with Churchill himself now at the helm (Chapter Six).

True, for those directly affected by the new weapons, these were horrific events, many saying later that they were most frightened by the 'deafening silence' which accompanied the V1's sometimes invisible death dive after the engine cut until the inevitable explosion. However, the author remembers that others simply went about their business, taking cover where they could only on hearing that distinctive sound peter out; indeed, after a time, many even failed to look up. Parliament attempted to calm Londoners, claiming that the weapon caused little more damage than the parachute mine used in the 1940 blitz, but it knew that the general public was becoming increasingly unnerved by the raids and that the rescue services were again sorely stretched. It was not only the civilians in the capital who were being affected; many servicemen, of all Allied nations, who were there seeking respite from front-line duties also suffered. Typically, at 08.00 on Monday 3 July (the day before American Independence Day), the US Army Club in Sloan Court was struck by a V1, leaving seventy-four servicemen and three civilians dead and fifty seriously wounded. It was small comfort for those who lived and worked in central London that the missiles lacked the necessary accuracy to home in on their aiming point (Tower Bridge), most being spread widely across Greater London and some falling as far south-east as Beneden, Kent, or well east in Billericay, Essex. By 2 August the V1s had killed 4,000 and left 14,000 injured.

The first V1 to fall in the author's area landed beside The Grange in Sewardstone, at 13.40 on Monday, 26 June. Chief Warden Ted Carter (Chapter Six) was on the spot in minutes, to find that the 'Fly' had destroyed much of the house and its contents, leaving the propulsion unit, still very hot, in a crater 4-feet deep and 10-feet in diameter. Two casualties were recovered and the ARP had the whole area cleared within an hour of the missile's impact – ready for the next one. They did not have long to wait; on 27 June another V1 landed on Lancaster Cottages, Avey Lane, Waltham Abbey, killing several cows sheltering from the rain in their shed, and this was quickly followed by another at Enfield Lock, where it killed four people and injured two more. So it went on, with increasing, if sporadic intensity – getting too close for comfort.

With 2,000 V1s having been launched from France by 29 June, personal tragedies abounded and rumours were

This photograph is believed to have been taken at Dartford, Greater London, in the early stages of the V1 campaign. (Author, Courtesy HTM Peenemünde)

One-hundred-and-twenty-one civilian and service worshippers were killed, and 68 seriously wounded, when the Guards Chapel on Birdcage Walk took a direct hit from a V1 during the Sunday morning service on 18 June. Only a small part of the Chapel could be incorporated in the new building shown here. (Author)

circulating that there was worse to come with a new and more devastating weapon. It has been claimed that all this was now causing the traditional British 'stiff upper lip' to sag, but the author cannot recall any overt sense of despair, especially with the imminent prospect of an advance by the Allies into the continent of Europe. True, many Londoners had suffered and were suffering, with 213 children killed and 500 injured by the V1s already, and there was again talk of evacuation, somewhat tempered when a V1 destroyed a fully-occupied evacuation centre at Westerham, Kent, on 30 June, which killed twenty-two children and eight nurses, underlining the need for evacuees to go much farther afield to escape errant V1s. In fact, a partial evacuation did go ahead on 5 July 1944, the second time in five years that bewildered children and some of their mothers were leaving their homes; so they went with no great enthusiasm. For the remainder, life went on more or less as usual, many cinemagoers staying in their seats when the screens showed a Doodlebug alert, and long weekend parties continued unabated, albeit with 'Doodlebug watchers' posted at high points nearby.

TOO CLOSE FOR COMFORT

As a schoolboy allowed to roam freely around rural Cheshunt and Waltham Holy Cross, on the northern outskirts of London, and throughout the capital itself, the author saw, heard and survived unscathed the onslaught by the flying bombs, as he had the blitz in 1940 and the 'baby blitz' of early 1944. He had watched the battles between the RAF and the mighty Luftwaffe raging overhead, day and night, and saw London burn, night after night, while multiple searchlights searched for the elusive bombers and the docile but dangerous barrage balloons waited for their prey, the whole scene set to the music of sirens, guns, bombs and the incessant clanging bells of the emergency vehicles. This was the 'London Concerto' of the time, and it would be performed many times, to different tunes in the next few months.

Peter Rooke, the head boy of the author's school at the time (Cheshunt Grammar School), and later a prominent local historian, added much to the V-weapons story in his *Cheshunt at War*. With the school having no dedicated shelter, the pupils were merely ordered to a strengthened centre lobby or to get under their desks, depending on how much warning they were given as the ominous sound approached – and there were some near misses. On 22 July the sirens wailed and the noise of a pulse jet ceased abruptly as the V1 crossed the Lea Valley and glided directly towards the school. As it did so it brushed the top of a tree in neighbouring Grundy Park, the explosion wrecking the park's sports pavilion but merely breaking a few classroom windows and depositing a large piece of timber onto the roof of the headmaster's car. As this was an airburst there was no crater, but the blast blew the leaves off several trees and stripped the bark of one, as it scattered large, tubular pieces of the bomb around the park.

Fate intruded again a few days later when the headmaster, Mr Moxom, decided that, with a slight lull in the hitherto almost continuous attacks, the end-of-term swimming gala should go ahead, as planned, at the nearby pool on the River Lea. The whole school mustered there just as the offensive resumed and a horrified Mr Moxom was forced to watch a V1 glide directly and silently towards the swimming pool – but it missed, to crash beyond the packed grandstand. This was all getting too close for comfort but, in the event, no school in the area suffered a direct hit and as time went on there was a noticeable tendency for many residents of the area to ignore the warnings, diving for cover only when the unmistakeable sound of a doodlebug's engine stopped. While the V1s were now getting most of the attention in and around London, the air continued to be full of other warlike noises, the author remembering the early morning of 5 August, the demented roar of an American B-24 Liberator as it skimmed the rooftops in

The V2 which came down at Chiswick, Greater London, at the start of the V2 offensive caused widespread damage. (Medmenham Collection)

A V1 struck trees off Honey Lane, Waltham Abbey, onto Larsen's Recreation Ground, where the author had been playing a little earlier. (Courtesy Janet Grove/ WAHS)

its death throes, before crashing in a nearby field on the A10, exploding on impact and killing all aboard. The bomber had collided with a B-17 Flying Fortress, which crashed elsewhere, both having been *en route* to the home of Hitler's *Vergeltungswaffen*.

V1s in flight kept everyone guessing: when would the engine stop – either to disrupt everyday life or fall harmlessly in open ground? On the afternoon of 17 August 1944, during their summer holiday, the author and his sister were rowing on Connaught Waters, Chingford, when a doodlebug passed over their heads, heading north-west, its engine shutting down shortly thereafter. They agreed that their house was in the firing line, but there was nothing they could do about it, and they were going to get their full two shillings worth on the water before making for home. Minutes later, Ted Carter, playing bowls in the Sports Field in Albury Ride spotted the same missile seemingly heading for Goffs Oak. They were all right, Ted later reporting that it had left 'an awful mess', with a crater in the middle of Goffs Lane, demolishing several small cottages, killing six of the residents and leaving twelve injured – but the boaters' house had survived.

The weather on 24 August was atrocious, with low cloud, poor visibility and drenching rain well into the night, as multiple V1s droned overhead

On 26 December 1944 a V2 destroyed the Prince of Wales public house on Mackenzie Road, Islington, which dated back to 1856, many customers enjoying the Christmas festivities being among the 68 fatalities. (Medmenham Collection)

Ted Carter and his wardens, invisible to them, the fighters and AA, and thus giving them a high degree of immunity, except from the radar-laid guns and balloons), again with those below left to guess where they would come down. One did come down on the fringe of the local area, at Holmwood Road, Enfield, Ted reporting that the darkness and heavy rain added to the chaos among the severely damaged houses, in a nightmare of 'dirt, muddle, and stink of leaking gas, wet sodden leaves, all set against the eerie light of the burning gas main', the cries of the injured and the wailing of sirens, in what had been, minutes before, a quiet little side-street'.

Understandably, the people of Cheshunt and Waltham Holy Cross kept repeating the question they had asked during the heavy bombing of 1940 and 1941: 'what were the Germans looking for in their area?' There were no significant military installations, so they could only assume that the bombers were targeting the Royal Gunpowder Mills, on the River Lea at the north-west corner of Waltham Abbey, but if so they were unlucky, with only one bomb exploding at the very northern tip of the site, without causing any damage or injury. In any event, the question was irrelevant in the V-weapons campaign, the missiles being too inaccurate to task against pin-point targets, they being aimed at central London (Tower Bridge) – some ten miles away.

On 20 September Warden Carter was soon on the scene again after a V1 ploughed into Cobbins Brook, on the edge of Larsen's Recreation Ground, Waltham Abbey, the author having left this favourite playground only a couple of hours before. The impact was at 21.35, and although there were no casualties, some 400 houses were damaged nearby. Again, there was much praise for the exemplary reaction of the ARP and local volunteers, in what was described as a copybook operation. The ARP were now well and truly rehearsed for this sort of eventuality.

From late August 1944 there had been a progressive reduction in the number of flying bombs reaching England, prompting Duncan Sandys to announce, on 7 September, that only sporadic raids by them could be expected thereafter, delivered mainly from the Heinkel bombers flying over the North Sea. He added that, in the past eighty days, 2,300 V1s had eluded the defences and reached Greater London, which had sustained 92 per cent of the fatal casualties caused by the V1s throughout England, but that the battle of the flying bombs was now all but over. They left a legacy; in addition to the all-pervading fatigue of war, the writer H.E. Bates reported that London and its people were now 'grey with the dust which hung over everything like a mask of death'. There were also rumours spreading throughout the country, perhaps stemming from – or surely encouraged by

Above and below: On Tuesday 2 January 1945, at 9.20 am, a V2 destroyed the Acorn Brush Factory in Swanfield Road, Waltham Cross, killing 7 and injuring 108. (Courtesy Daphne Rooke)

German propaganda – that members of the Royal Family had been killed, Buckingham Palace had been destroyed, 600 flying bombs per day had pounded the capital and that poison gas had been used; above all, that there was more to come, with the addition of a new and more powerful weapon. Other than the latter threat, none of this was true, but morale did suffer, there was a rise in the criticism of national defence. Sadly, V1 attacks had not ended, and the time had come for the V2 rockets to join the party.

At 18.43 on 8 September an enormous explosion destroyed the tranquillity of that late summer evening, followed by a short rushing sound and a second bang, signalling that a rocket had passed through the transonic zone, just before the first V2 to arrive in Britain struck Chiswick, in west London. Sixteen seconds later, a second rocket fell harmlessly in Epping Long Green, shaking windows and doors in nearby Waltham Abbey. At first, Chief Warden Ted Carter believed this to be the 'rumble and echo' of approaching thunder and went on picking apples in his garden, but after a few 'phone calls it was clear that the V2 offensive had begun. Accompanied by Wardens Ellis and Smith, Ted made his way through Epping Forest to Parndon Wood, where they found a crater, 8-feet deep and 20-feet in diameter, surrounded by a mass of light alloy fragments. The size of the crater was not surprising, given that the V2 weighed some 13 tons, had a one-ton warhead of Amatol high explosive, and that its near vertical, supersonic dive gave it a terminal velocity of some 3,000 mph.

The government had expected rocket attacks on England, but kept this from the public, and continued to do so well after the first V2s had landed in England, by perpetuating the myth that the sudden explosions were nothing more than 'exploding gas mains'. Such stories held little water, especially among those on the receiving end of the new weapon, also because there were so many of such incidents and because the German public radio was proclaiming the success of rockets which would 'bring London to its knees' – so eventually the government had to come clean. By then every V2 which landed in England, or just off the coast, was being given a 'Big Ben' number, thirty-six being listed in September 1944, ninety-five in October and 150 in November.

The second rocket to hit the author's district, arrived at Goose Green, Hoddesdon, on 5 October, and the third, on Sunday, 12 November, found its way to the middle of St Leonard's Road, Nazing. This was the worst V2 incident locally, to date, destroying a small hamlet of cottages, close to where the author was visiting his uncle at Monkham's estate. Ted Carter remembers the very sorry sight of workers from all the emergency services

Above and previous: The worst destruction caused by a V2 in the author's area occurred on 7 March 1945 when a V2 impacted on Highbridge Road, the only direct route between Waltham Cross and Waltham Abbey, and close to where the author had been fishing on the River Lea only a short time before. Four people were killed and 53 injured. (Courtesy Janet Grove/WAHS)

Smithfield Meat Market and Farringdon Railway Station, below, suffered extensive damage and over 150 fatal casualties from a V2 on 8 March 1945. (Courtesy Janet Grove/WAHS)

A V2 ended its days at the confluence of Bury Green Road, Cromwell Road and Churchgate on Sunday afternoon 14 January 1945, breaking all the windows on the south side of St Mary's Church where 100 children were attending Sunday School. (Courtesy Janet Grove/WAHS)

and local civilians ploughing their way through the rubble, searching for casualties, finally to recover ten bodies and many injured.

Farther afield, and arguably the worst V2 incident in London, occurred at New Cross, Lewisham, at 12.26 on 25 November, when a V2 demolished Woolworth's and the next door Co-op Stores, both packed with people, the former said to have 'bulged outwards before imploding', the passengers in a passing bus and army lorry also adding to the 168 deaths and 121 seriously injured. Debris scattered between the Town Hall and New Cross Station took three hectic days to clear.

Christmas Day 1944 was quiet, with no missiles reported over London, but Boxing Day saw another major tragedy caused by a V2 which fell beside a pub on Mackenzie Road, Islington, at 21.26, at the height of the festivities, causing the floor to collapse and throwing many of the revellers into the cellar below. To make matters worse, the freezing conditions and heavy fog hampered rescue and recovery, with ice having to be smashed to reach the water needed to douse several fires. Firemen and rescue teams toiled well beyond dawn on the following day, having had to tunnel into the cellar with great care, for fear that more of the building would collapse. Sixty-eight people died there that night, and hundreds more were injured.

On 2 January 1945 the author was nearby again, looking over a wall from Cedar's Park, watching the trains go by on a branch line from Cheshunt to Enfield, when a massive explosion rent the air over Swanfield Road, Waltham Cross, as the Acorn Brush Factory disappeared in a cloud of dust and flame. There having been no warning, this was clearly another V2. Help appeared at once, from all directions, as if well-choreographed, and Ted Carter was among them. He helped load the dead and wounded into ambulances, and recalls the sight of a very brave woman, a factory clerk, standing on a box, 'herself cut, bleeding and dirty, calling the roll and ticking the names as the survivors answered'. Ted said that this was 'the biggest, dirtiest incident he had seen to so far', with seven killed and 108 injured.

There was another serious V2 incident in Cheshunt at 15.30 on the afternoon of 14 January when a rocket landed on the junction of College Road and Bury Green Road leading to the cemetery. Several people had just alighted there from a No.242 bus to Cuffley, and two of those killed were visiting the grave of their daughter, who had died in the mayhem at the Acorn Factory two weeks before. Two other adults, again bound for the cemetery, were also killed and several buildings suffered considerable damage, while two children of the Thompson family, who were only 50 yards from the rocket when it exploded, were badly injured, one of whom died later in hospital. A little farther up Bury Green Road, the Misses Butler and Smerdon, two of the author's schoolteachers, seemed completely unperturbed by the chaos around them, but had to decline advice to have 'a nice cup of tea', because there was no longer any water or gas on tap. Slivers of shattered glass from all the windows on the south side of St Mary's Church, in College Road, could also have hurt many of the 100 children at Sunday School there, but miraculously, they all escaped without a scratch, and after a suitable prayer departed to their homes.

The author's last close shave was at 17.00 on Wednesday 7 March 1945 when a V2 landed on Highbridge Street, the only road between Waltham Cross to Waltham Abbey, igniting fires and leaving a very deep crater some 75 feet in diameter, which immediately filled with water from severed sewage pipes, all telephone lines, gas and electricity supplies also being destroyed. The local ARP and rescue services were quick to react, the wardens setting up control points and incident rooms, while the NFS provided emergency field telephones, but it would be some time before any motor vehicles could drive around the crater between the two towns. Additional help homed in from Cheshunt and Chigwell, the WVS provided meals and mobile canteens did a roaring trade all the following day, while unsafe buildings were demolished and work began to restore the utilities and services. Meanwhile an enthusiastic bulldozer driver, while attempting to create a temporary road through the debris, ventured too close to the water-filled crater – and toppled in.

An hour earlier, the author had been fishing on the River Lea, 200 yards from the impact point, and was there again the next day to see a scene of well-organised activity and major changes to the local landscape. A wardens' post had disappeared completely and many properties both sides of the road, including the Alms Houses, the County Court, the Home Guard Drill Hall and the Ordnance Arms had been badly damaged, some irreparably. This was to be the worst and last V2 incident in the Waltham Holy Cross district, leaving a great deal of damage, four dead and sixty-three injured.

A day later, and with only three weeks to go before the end of the rocket attacks, Central London also had its most serious V2 incident. London's Smithfield Meat Market and Farrington Street railway station took a direct hit at 11.30, in the middle of a busy market day, the rocket smashing through the massive concrete and steel structure onto the railway loading bays below, killing 110 people and leaving countless more injured. A large number of women and children were said to have been within that number, it having been rumoured that rabbits might be on sale there that day.

The last rocket came down at Orpington on 27 March, killing Mrs Ivy Millichamp, the last person to die from the V-weapons and, early on the following morning, the last flying bomb landed at Claverhambury, near Waltham Holy Cross, Ted Carter again being among the first to find the crater, but with very little surrounding damage and no injuries. It was over.

All those who endured the sleepless nights and disruption of the Luftwaffe's flying-bomb offensive will remember the ominous sound of their arrival, and that they were relatively safe while the noise continued. Some, particularly those who had survived a near miss, took to their shelters, conscious of the danger that one ton of high explosives could cause with blast, cratering and fragmentation. Others, and there were many of them, became a little blasé, unwisely tending to play a game of 'cat and mouse' with Hitler's new killing machines as they proliferated – and perhaps paying the ultimate penalty. It was different with the V2 rockets, which gave no warning, and the majority in the land became fatalistic, accepting that there was nothing practical they could do to avoid the

Above and below: The author and his wife inspect the work done to make a fishing lake at Galley Hill, Waltham Abbey, from the crater caused by the last V1 to land in their area on 12 July 1944. (Author)

cruelty they inflicted, and rising to every occasion with strenuous rescue, recovery and rehabilitation efforts. As with the London blitz, each found their own way of dealing with the onslaught. While the people of Cheshunt and Waltham Holy Cross suffered far less than many in other districts in and around Greater London, they saw, heard and were able to sense what others had been going through but, even for them, this final intrusion on their lives had been too close for comfort.

Chapter 8

Codename 'Crossbow'

The UK active and passive defences did their best to protect the British homeland against the flying bombs and to mitigate their effects, but they could never do enough – and they were impotent against the rockets. Fortunately, wise heads had realised that, in accordance with the time-honoured adage, that 'offence is (often) the best means of defence', action had to be taken against the enemy's design, development and testing installations in their heartland, together with any production and logistics centres and launching sites, there and in enemy-occupied countries. The purely air defence assets have been outlined in the previous chapter, but in the context of a campaign against the V-weapons, the offensive assets would include heavy and medium bombers, fighter-bombers, all air reconnaissance forces and, later in the war, the tactical air power of the Allied Air Expeditionary Force (AAEF).

In 1943 the clear need for a central body to co-ordinate all matters pertaining to Germany's long-range weapons led to the formation of a committee initially comprising politicians, appropriate scientists, military and associated specialists, chaired by the controversial Duncan Sandys (Chapter Four), working under the code name 'Bodyline'. Inevitably, with main players such as Sandys, Lord Cherwell, R.V. Jones, the intelligence community, particularly Bletchley Park and 'Bimbo' Norman, and the Air Ministry operational staffs, there were tensions from the start, leading to several changes at the helm, representation and access to highly classified information.

On 15 November 1943 Bodyline gave way to a new codename, Crossbow, their activities coming later under the popular heading of Operation CROSSBOW (best known for the film of that name). The Crossbow Committee would be a sub-committee of the JIC, with its own directorate in the Air Ministry. Carrying on the work of Bodyline, the Crossbow Committee set about re-evaluating all the intelligence available, and demanding further contributions to it, for a continuing assessment by experts to determine the exact nature of these weapons, the threats they posed and when they might be used in anger, thereafter to consider further offensive and defensive countermeasures against them. Typically, throughout its evolution, Bodyline and Crossbow would take inputs from or involve the Foreign Office, the War Office through MI 10 (Weapons and Technical Analysis), the Military Intelligence Germany (Technical) Branch, and the Directorate of Prisoners of War (PoW).

For all who wished to see it, there was an abundance of evidence, from multiple sources (Chapter Four), that Germany was well advanced in the development of at least two long-range missiles, the V1 flying bomb and the V2 rocket, the like of which had not been seen before on a battlefield. Moreover, it was becoming clear that London, and perhaps the invasion ports in southern England, were primary targets. So it was that the Peenemünde research and development complex and the huge construction programme underway in north-west France, clearly designated as the main launch area for both missiles targeting London, were of particular interest.

By mid-1943 it had become clear that Peenemünde was at the very roots of the burgeoning threat from long-range rockets and flying bombs and the War Cabinet Defence Committee directed that key elements of a huge and rapidly developing facility should be destroyed by RAF Bomber Command in a maximum effort at the earliest opportunity. The Commander-in-Chief (C-in-C) RAF Bomber Command, Air Chief Marshal Sir Arthur Harris, was not happy; he saw this as a major distraction from his preference for 'carpet-bombing' German cities, in which he aimed to create as much destruction and panic as possible, disrupting industrial facilities and the associated infrastructure, but he was also concerned about the practicalities of the task. His bombers would be operating at extreme ranges, where their new navigation aid, Oboe, could also be unreliable, while the bombing aid H2S would not be sufficiently accurate for the precision required. This would be the first time that Bomber Command had carried out a mass attack of this nature against relatively small target nodes, in which precise navigation and bomb-aiming would be essential, so the raid would have to be carried out on a clear, moonlight night, sadly when they would be at their most vulnerable to the Luftwaffe's fighters.

Bomber Command assigned all its suitable assets to the task in the hope of achieving the aim in one blow, and to reduce the risk of interference by enemy fighters, high speed Mosquito bombers would carry out a diversionary raid, dropping Window to confuse the radar by simulating a major raid on Berlin. Also, because this would be the first, major precision raid at night, Pathfinder bombers and a Master Bomber would mark crucial aiming points and then remain in the local area to give directions and corrections. The Peenemünde raid was scheduled for the night of 17/18 August 1943 under a full moon in a cloudless sky. This wholly British effort would involve a mixed force of 596 bombers from fifty-four Bomber Command squadrons, led by a Stirling of No.90 Squadron based at West Wickham, flown by Flight Lieutenant George Crew. They would seek to unload 1,650 tons of high explosive bombs and 274 tons of incendiaries on Peenemünde East, specifically the experimental station, the rocket factory and the specialist workers' quarters, as recommended by Duncan Sandys. Interestingly, the massive, very visible coal-fired power station, which served the whole complex, was not on the target list and remains intact to this day. Neither was the Luftwaffe airfield, the V1 test site nor the Me163 rocket fighter and Me262 jet fighter development facility at Peenemünde West – no doubt a matter of regret to those bomber crews who were to suffer from these innovative aircraft later in the war. R.V. Jones had not been consulted on aiming points and was not happy with the selection.

Group Captain John Searby, CO of No.83 Squadron, would lead the Pathfinders, acting as the Master Bomber and, for the first time, a number of 'shifters' were employed, their purpose being to re-direct the marker flares, if required, as the raid progressed. There would be three waves of bombers, the last employing the 'time and distance' procedure for finding their target from a clearly visible run-in point. Four Mosquito bomber squadrons would provide the diversionary force, approaching Berlin via Denmark, in an attempt to draw away the Luftwaffe fighters.

Initially, the raid was proclaimed a success. Twenty-five buildings were said to have been destroyed within the experimental works, including the drawing office, while the V2 assembly shop had received a direct hit which destroyed valuable documents and records, and caused the death of Dr Walter Thiel, the chief rocket propulsion engineer. Production was said to have been delayed by two to six months, depending on the source of these estimates. However, some 600 foreign workers were also killed, including several invaluable informants, while many of the German specialists who had been targeted survived, and heroic action among the German survivors saved volumes of vital documents. With HYDRA having been only partially successful, it was clear that further raids on Peenemünde would be necessary.

Forty-one bombers were lost in the raid, and to this day part of the fuselage of one remains visible in the lake close to Peenemünde village; the third wave suffered most, the Mosquito diversion having played itself out in time for the fighters to re-muster over Usedom and catch their adversaries as they departed for home. The fighters included Bf110s converted to fire twin *Schrage Musik*, angled-upward-firing cannon, into the bombers' bellies, and it is they who might have accounted for six of the last wave.

As with Peenemünde, the potential missile launch sites in France had, for some months in 1943, been under continuous surveillance from the air, enabling the Central Interpretation Unit (CIU) at Medmenham to confirm connections between the two. Moreover, the photographic imagery did much to support information from Allied agents on the ground in France that the Germans were building installations which could only have been destined for the rocket and or flying bombs. These included eight big hardened facilities and an increasing number of storage and ski sites for launching V1s, whose launching ramps were all pointing towards London. Where photo cover was lacking, the PRU was tasked to fill in the gaps.

Then began a debate on the best time and means of attacking each target array. It was agreed that, in general, the sites should be struck just before their completion, that the accuracy expected from medium-level bombing would not be good enough, that 'area bombing' from high level (weather permitting) might be profitable, but that the preferred solution was pinpoint attacks by fighter-bombers.

The RAF's No.2 Group, Second Tactical Air Force (2TAF), commanded by Air Vice Marshal Basil Embry, had already been hard at it. At the end of October 1943, No.2 Group had struck eighty-eight known ski sites, and was ready to attack another fifty, yet to be confirmed. In the next six months the group's Typhoons, Spitfires, Marauders, Bostons and Mitchells contributed to the total of 4,710 sorties flown by all Allied units against V-weapon targets, usually carrying out their attacks in fair weather only, for fear of collateral damage in the occupied countries. They faced little opposition from enemy fighters, but a vast array of mixed AA took its toll, or at least distracted the bomber and fighter-bomber pilots from their aim as they ran into their targets. Attempts to delay construction work at the launch sites included attacks on the Todt Administration Building in Audinghen on 25 November, 2 Group Spitfires leaving only a few buildings standing before they themselves were attacked by Bf109s. On the afternoon of 26 November, 2 Group medium bombers flew 119 sorties over Martinvast, losing three Mitchells to AA, while Typhoons and Spitfires, flying top cover, accounted for a number of Fw190s. Many BODYLINE/CROSSBOW targets survived the end of 1943 because of poor weather, but in that final month small raids were still possible against Drionville, Heuringham, Puchervin, St Pierre des Jonquières, le Mesnil Alard, Pommereval, la Glacerie, Bois de Capelle, Crecy, Yvrenche and Ligescourt. Again, AA of all calibres was particularly heavy at all heights, and on 21 December Spitfires jousted with forty Fw190s, shooting down three of the enemy for the loss of one of their own. Two days later an experimental raid by thirty-six Bostons of 2 Group was carried out at low level, for which the crews were not trained; it was not a success and was not repeated.

The higher performance Mosquitos from RAF Sculthorpe which had also joined the BODYLINE force in November proved more successful at low level, and could operate in poorer weather without the fighter protection needed by the medium bombers. To further minimise their losses, they would fly over the sea at the lowest practical level, climb to 4,000 feet over the coastal defences and then dive back to low level, albeit with the difficulty of acquiring their targets at the last moment, or carried out dive attacks from 1,500 feet. Alternatively, they would approach at 11,000 feet, in order to acquire their targets early, then dive down to 6,000 feet to deliver their bombs, achieving very good errors errors of only 150 feet, but this tactic was possible only in good weather and it meant risking greater exposure to air defence and gun radars. So it was that ultra-low level attacks remained the preferred option.

While CROSSBOW continued to be a major priority in 1944, it would compete with the needs of the forthcoming invasion of the continent, and this brought about a re-organisation of the wing structures at the 2 Group airfields of Lasham, Hunsdon, Hertford Bridge and Dunsfold, these wings being designated for early deployment to the continent.

The Americans now deplored what they believed to be wasted effort on CROSSBOW targets, tensions between the two nations increasing, with the Americans now demanding more access to intelligence on the suspected missiles which they believed they were being denied, making this a pre-condition for any further material help in CROSSBOW. There was also a suspicion that some ski sites were now no more than a cunning deception, to lure Allied aircraft into 'flak-traps', and they could have been right; the Germans had left some abandoned sites fully exposed, even occupying them with skeleton staff to draw off the bombers from the new 'modified' sites they were developing. So it was that, from January 1944, the British passed on to the Americans their perceived threats to the UK from flying bombs and rockets, with details on some of the ski sites in France, whereupon the USAAF carried out a raid by 1,300 heavy bombers, with a fighter escort, dropping 1,700 tons of bombs on twenty-three ski sites (now known as 'Noball' targets), and destroying three. In the more constructive bi-lateral talks which followed there was general agreement that the missiles might threaten the forthcoming invasion of the continent, not sufficient to postpone the operation but enough to justify the joint effort against CROSSBOW targets to continue. The Americans then asked why the Germans would spend so much energy and scarce resources on a (V2) rocket, if it contained only a small, high-explosive warhead; could it be that the beleaguered nation had a low yield atomic or, more likely, a bacteriological warhead in mind, such as the Americans themselves had been considering? They were certainly aware of bacteria yeast. With such questions unanswered, the case for continuing to target the V2s prevailed.

Having been convinced that their invasion forces might be attacked by the V-weapons, the Americans went one step further, arranging for a professor from Princeton University, Bob Robertson, to meet R.V. Jones in London to learn more about the threats and discuss a joint approach against them. The meeting went well, Robertson returning to the USA to make the case for all-out American support for CROSSBOW. Their first contribution was to examine the best way of dealing with the 'bunker sites', such as le Blockhaus d'Éperlecques at Watten, in the Pas de Calais. General Grandison Gardner, commander of the Army Air Force Proving Ground at Eglin Field, Florida, was ordered to build an accurate mock-up of a site 'within days'. This he did, and in the following month Air Marshal Sir Norman Bottomley and Air Vice Marshal Frank Inglis, representing the RAF's operational and intelligence interests respectively, were invited to Eglin to discuss the best means of attacking such a target, the seismic effects of the British 12,000lb Tallboy bomb coming into the discussion. The VIPs then witnessed an impressive demonstration of a TV guided bomb, dropped from high level by a Flying Fortress, striking its target – but no such weapon would be ready for operational use in the war. Following additional trials at Eglin, General Gardner recommended that the low-level approach by fighter-bombers was the most effective means of attacking the V1 ski sites and modified sites – and so it would prove. While the debate continued, heavy and medium bombers kept up their assault on the bunker sites, fighter-bombers the redundant ski and elusive modified sites. On 4 March General Eisenhower approved a plan which served both Operation OVERLORD and the continued campaign against the flying-bomb sites, with the flexibility to switch forces rapidly from one priority to the other. In April 1944 the Allies effort against CROSSBOW targets got more than its share, peaking at 4,100 sorties to deliver 7,500 tons of conventional ordnance, and detailed plans were drawn up for the use of chemical stores, should retaliation in kind be necessary. The USAAF was also contributing more to the reconnaissance programme, looking especially for the modified sites, the aircrew and PIs no longer so easily taken in by the deception measures being adopted by the Germans.

While it had little new to go on, the Air Ministry predicted that an offensive by flying bombs against England might now begin at the end of March 1944, and that, in the first fifteen days of such an attack, 160 tons of high explosives might be spread across Greater London in 10 to 12 hours, recurring after 48 hr intervals. In that this would equate to separate raids carried out by twenty Lancasters, it was relatively good news – and it could be even better depending on the effectiveness of England's defensive screen and on the success of attacks against the launch sites. The bad news was that Bletchley Park was reporting general improvements in the accuracy of the bombs on trials in the Baltic, Jones estimating that some 40 per cent of those launched might reach London, and intelligence sources had yet to be fully aware of the potential of the modified sites springing up, largely unobserved, within reach of London. The SIS and Bletchley Park were also busy keeping a watching brief on Wachtel's *Flakgruppe Creil*, the elusive Wachtel himself (alias Wolf) plying continuously between Zempin, Paris, and his units throughout northern France.

On the night of 13/14 June the first V1 fell on England (Chapter Seven) but the government said nothing publically until forced to do so and three days later the centre of London came under heavy attack, the tragic destruction of the Guards Chapel in Wellington Barracks bringing a flurry of activity, including a hastily convened meeting of the Crossbow Committee. It was a measure of the importance

Results of an Allied raid on Engine Test Stand XI, Peenemünde West. (Medmenham Collection)

130

Peenemünde after
Bomber Command raid
on 18 August 1944.
(Medmenham Collection)

Winston Churchill attached to the work of the committee, that he himself took the chair in the immediate wake of the Guards Chapel disaster (Chapter Seven) until his involvement with OVERLORD became overwhelming and, to the dismay of many, he handed the role back to Sandys. Bletchley Park reacted by instituting new procedures for the circulation of sensitive intelligence; Professor Norman and Dr R.V. Jones remained primary recipients, as did the Air Ministry, but other ministries and interested parties were omitted. Although a wider distribution followed numerous complaints, it was subject to conditions and reservations in attempts to keep a close rein on who knew what, and to withhold from Sandys some details on the A4 (V2). The committee met again on 22 June to dwell primarily on the likely functions of the huge hardened sites at Wizernes, Watten, Siracourt and Mymoyecques, and again whether the expensive 12,000lb Tallboy (seismic) bombs should be used against them. The committee heard little new on the rocket, although many were aware that a great deal of convincing evidence on the V2 had come from Helmut Müller, a rocket specialist captured in Italy and interrogated very successfully at Trent Park.

The Crossbow Committee then came under fire for not predicting the start of the flying-bomb offensive, for failing to provide clarity on the command and control, associated intelligence and communications organisation of the German missile deployments, and there were those who were wondering whether Air Commodore Colin Grierson, Director of Special Operations, the man directly responsible for CROSSBOW operations, was now the right man for the job, and in early July, he was relieved of his responsibilities for collating intelligence, that job then going to R.V. Jones, who would also assist in the preparation of the target list, from an office in the Air Ministry. Jones and his new deputy, Wing Commander John Mapplebeck from Bletchley Park, would also work closely with a new army/air cell, responsible for monitoring all aspects of the rocket story. There were also questions on the commitment of nearly half of the total bombing capacity to CROSSBOW, given that there was so little to show for it, the Americans again becoming very unhappy with the CROSSBOW targeting and now making it clear that they would much prefer to 'go it alone'. Rather than the many futile attempts to find and destroy the obscure, highly mobile modified launch sites, their preference was to attack the German factories making the V1s' gyro guidance systems back in Germany and the large storage depots which had been positively identified at Saint-Lô, St-Leu d'Esserent, Nucourt and Rilly la Montagne, together with the means of transport from these depots to the front line and, by July, the USAAF heavy bombers were targeting the hydrogen peroxide (V1 fuel) production centres. Acting on the advice from the Enemy Objectives Unit (EOU), General Spaatz, commanding the US Strategic Air Forces in Europe took the case to the Supreme Commander, General Eisenhower, but lost. On the day the 2,000th V1 was launched from the Pas de Calais, Eisenhower found in favour of a recommendation by his RAF deputy, Air Marshal Sir Arthur Tedder, that raids on the V1 launch and logistic sites should continue to be the priority and the RAF continued to bomb storage depots found in the Oise Valley, sadly with heavy losses.

Towards the end of June 1944 tensions had also increased within the ministries in London and operational staffs, with Sandys attempting to get rid of Air Marshal Sir Roderick Hill, Air Officer Commanding, ADGB, allegedly for showing too much loyalty to his fighter pilots against the interests of General Pile's AA gunners, at a time when neither fighters nor guns were achieving what was needed of them. To add to the defenders' woes, the flying bombs were now appearing from over the Thames estuary, running into London from east to west, being launched from the Luftwaffe's bombers, demanding a rearrangement of the available defences. Moreover, the British public sensed that the much vaunted bombing campaign against the V-weapon sites in France and associated targets was doing too little to protect them, and were outraged at the indiscriminate use of such missiles against them, tempting the Prime Minister to 'flatten', a selected list of German cities in retaliation. He also called on his ministers and military chiefs to consider again the selective use of poison gas, chemical and or germ agents, such as anthrax – with maximum ferocity and without moral qualms. However, on both counts he was persuaded to hold fire, lest the Germans themselves had something more evil up their sleeves as reprisals – gas attacks and rockets being the fears. He did now decide that the basic facts about the V-weapons should be brought into the public domain and, in a carefully worded address to Parliament on 6 July, he stressed the achievements of the Allied intelligence and combat forces. He claimed that only one person was being killed for every one flying bomb, but that another weapon, probably a rocket with greater destructive potential could be in the offing. There was no doubting his frustration that the military and the intelligence services could not find more of the highly elusive modified sites, or discover definitive information on the stratospheric rockets, now known to be undergoing trials. As for Lord Cherwell, he had been proved wrong over the Doodlebugs and, despite R.V. Jones's protestations, he was still pouring scorn on the likelihood of successful rocket attacks.

Above and prevoius spreed: RAF and USAAF heavy bombers were used extensively against V1 and V2 sites in the Pas de Calais region. (Mimoyecques Museum and Medmenham Collection)

On 6 July Air Vice Marshal Frank Inglis, Assistant Chief of the Air Staff Intelligence, and those cleared to access Ultra information, welcomed Lieutenant Colonel Stewart McClintic, the deputy intelligence chief of the US Strategic Air Forces, to the Air Ministry. McClintic would be the American spokesman on any retaliatory measures against the missiles, and at this meeting he was promised full and timely access to all CROSSBOW intelligence. This small gesture did little to satisfy the increasingly frustrated Americans, who sought an equal share of the decision-making in a joint committee, comprising three British and three American intelligence and operational specialists, to be responsible for collecting, analysing and disseminating all CROSSBOW intelligence, for the most expeditious employment of the weapons available. They would eventually get their way, with a newly formed Anglo-American

CODENAME 'CROSSBOW'

Joint Crossbow Target Priorities Committee holding its inaugural meeting in London on 21 July. It did not go well, Mr Churchill clearly identifying the RAF as the lead player and leaving the Americans feeling like second-class citizens, with advisory powers only. General Spaatz's spokesman, Colonel Hughes, called again for the committee to have a more comprehensive remit, a lack of the necessary information to do so again being a major complaint, and again the Americans got their way. At the next meeting a consensus agreed that all raids on the ski sites should cease, modified sites should be subjected to harassment only and there should be no more 'dumb bombing' of the bunker sites. On getting to hear of the Committee's deliberations, Sandys attempted to get a seat at that table, but a consensus among his superiors decided that he had enough to do dispensing intelligence, and that he should not become involved in 'operations'.

Among the many types of offensive aircraft employed against the missile sites in France were the B-26 Marauders of the USAAF's 9th Air Force, based in Britain. They were used predominantly in daylight raids, to good effect and with some success against the Luftwaffe fighters, working in close formation flights of four aircraft to make best use of their collective heavy gun armament. However, in the summer of 1944 two B-26 Groups, the 322nd at Andrewsfield, and the 323rd at Earls Colne, were tasked to evaluate the use of their aircraft against CROSSBOW targets at night, thus forfeiting their ideal defensive formations. At night, they were ordered to operate in a stream of single aircraft behind a pathfinder which would mark the intended target with flares, on which the following crews should release their bombs. Initially they were successful, but the Germans soon caught on to their tactics and, on their third mission, against Château de Ribeaucourt, northern France, on the night of 7/8 July, they suffered heavily from the moment they crossed the coast into the Pas de Calais, from well-co-ordinated searchlights, AA and night-fighter defences. The two groups continued to practise night operations for the remainder of 1944, with varying results, until it was concluded that night operations achieved little more than could be accomplished by day.

On 11 July the rocket threat was the main subject for discussion at a meeting of the scientific, intelligence and military heads in London, who called for every effort to be made to obtain the fragments of the V2 which had landed in Sweden, and five days later, small but significant pieces of the rocket arrived aboard the Mosquito. These revealed some very important features, particularly on the means of lubricating the moving parts, that two sets of diametrically-opposed pairs of guide vanes operated in the jet flow, to provide guidance in azimuth and elevation, with gyroscopes to provide stability, the very complex wiring, clues on the missile's fuel and evidence that it was designed for mass production. This information was gratefully received by the scientists and released to the War Cabinet meeting on 18 July. It was at this meeting that R.V. Jones made his debut as the new authority for the dissemination of all intelligence on the long-range missile threat, and he reported that photographic reconnaissance had confirmed the presence of V2 rockets at Blizna.

Blizna had become another potential, if short-lived, source of the final pieces of the V2 jigsaw and Churchill wrote to Moscow, perhaps in hope more than expectation, that Marshal Stalin would order an immediate search of the Blizna range area as soon as it was occupied to look for more tell-tale fragments of the German missiles, and allow a British team to join the search (Chapter Four). Towards the end of July Ultra intelligence on Blizna was drying up in the face of the Russian advance and the last V2 was fired there on 24 July, before the units moved to a new testing site at Tucheler Heide, in West Prussia, with its impact area 150 miles south. Meanwhile, more details on the rocket were coming in from agents in France who found what they believed were launching platforms built into existing roads, and from Polish partisans who had captured, examined and hidden an errant V2 in Poland (vide Operation WILDHORN- Chapter Four).

Sandys lamented his loss of authority and believed that he was also being denied information he needed to fulfil his new responsibilities. He felt sure that the Air Ministry was denying him critical information from prisoners captured in Normandy, photographs from Blizna and from Normandy of the concrete plinths believed to be the launch pads for the rockets, and details on the way LXV Corps would be co-ordinating V1 and V2 operations. Gradually, however, perhaps with a little help from his father-in-law, the prime minister, Sandys began getting more of the information he sought, even from that most sacred Most Secret Source (MSS). On 25 July he presented his latest report to the War Cabinet Crossbow Committee, reiterating that the V2's warhead was likely to contain between 5 to 10 tons of high explosive (R.V. Jones now thought it might be as low as one ton), that the rocket needed no special launch facilities, was likely to be radio controlled in the initial stages of flight and that it was most probably fuelled by liquid oxygen and ethyl alcohol. He thought that at least 1,000 units might be available already but that there was no evidence of the rockets being moved forward to their launch sites.

That afternoon, at a War Cabinet meeting, the Prime Minister and Home Secretary Morrison were given to believe that the V2s were all but ready to deploy, that the deployment and launching would be relatively simple and that the rocket sites were well within range of Britain's capital, but they again expressed their disappointment over some lack of clarity on the weapons themselves. It was then that Duncan Sandys began to flex his muscles again, suggesting, *inter alia,* that immediate consideration be given to bombing the production centres for liquid oxygen (the rocket's fuel), to which end he presented the Air Ministry with a list of these centres. This action would, of course, have no immediate effect on the offensive which now seemed imminent.

At the end of a very busy July Frank Inglis removed Dr R.V. Jones from his post as Assistant Director Intelligence (Science), replacing him with Air Commodore Jack Easton, Director of Intelligence (Research), as his man on the Crossbow Committee, tasking him with an urgent review of the distribution of such intelligence as was essential for external agencies to fulfil their respective responsibilities. While Jones returned to his duties with the SIS, he remained a member of the War Cabinet Crossbow Committee, and still had access to highly secret material at Bletchley and Medmenham. While no doubt aggrieved, he made it known that he would continue to watch developments with the rocket, and report accordingly. Sandys' reaction to all this was mixed; his *bête noire,* Jones, would no longer be in the Air Ministry to irritate him but he was still no nearer to the 'inner circle' of intelligence recipients; Lord Cherwell and Jones had helped to see to that.

Despite the acrimony of who should know what, the full story on the V2 was now emerging, the War Cabinet Crossbow Committee Meeting on 10 August accepting R.V. Jones's latest assessment that the V2 had a warhead of a ton, although it wondered again how Hitler could justify the enormous expenditure on such a relatively low-yield weapon – had they missed something? Although equally puzzled, R.V. Jones suggested that it might simply be an illustration of German pride in such a masterly innovation while harbouring an outlandish hope that the V2, coupled with the V1, might persuade the Allies to come to terms

The debate on CROSSBOW target priorities also continued to be controversial, with old and new, objective and subjective inputs competing, and specific agreements in short supply; but a target list drafted on 10 August concentrated on liquid oxygen plants and the transport system, predominantly in Belgium. The committee then considered again how to

Above and left: Wizernes V2 Bunker under construction and after a raid, 6 July 1944. (Medmenham Collection)

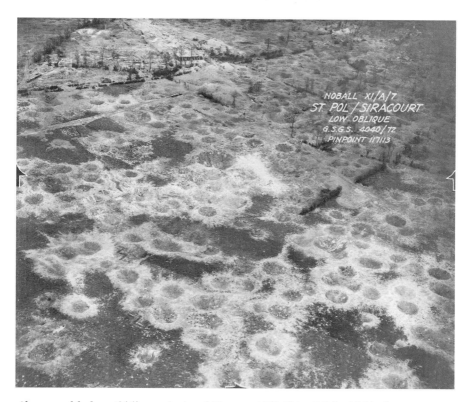

Above and below: Oblique photo of Siracourt V1 Site, 7 July 1944, the town now totally rebuilt following carpet bombing. (Medmenham Collection and Author)

Left and below: A vertical photo of Watten V2 site, taken in 1943, and now, showing critical damage from Allied bombing. (Medmenham Collection and Author)

arrest or at least restrict the massive output of both missiles from the main production centre, Mittelwerk, deep underground in the Harz Mountains, mostly out of sight from the air, with little more than rail lines protruding from the mountain. The USAAF is believed to have given some thought to repetitive blocking of the tunnel entrances and causing destructive fires locally, but this would have required very accurate bombing and would have placed many PoWs and other foreign workers at risk, and no reports can be found that such missions went ahead.

Two more Crossbow Committee meetings followed on 25 August, at one of which a recently-captured senior German officer revealed the intention to begin the rocket campaign in mid-September, and Lieutenant Colonel Pryor, of MI14, warned that there might be no other tell-tale warnings before then. The following day a stubborn and resilient R.V. Jones circulated a paper containing every important aspect of rocket intelligence, together with a long list of suggested targets. This *magnum opus* did him little good; his successor, Wing Commander John Mapplebeck, had already taken his place, and on 27 August, Air Vice Marshal Inglis told him that the Chief of the Air Staff, Marshal of the Royal Air Force Sir Charles Portal had ordered that all the copies of his paper be withdrawn forthwith.

As the talking went on, so did the Allied bombing, albeit without full agreement on priorities. The US 8th Air Force had attacked Peenemünde on 18 July, and did so again on 4 August and 25 August, while striking targets around Nordhausen and five liquid oxygen plants in Belgium and northern France. Among its strategic targets Bomber Command struck the Adam Opel AG, the automobile works suspected of being involved with the missiles. Attacks were also carried on V1 *Feldmunitionslager* (munitions depots) and launch sites by medium bombers and fighter-bombers, until it was accepted that they were achieving little, while causing considerable collateral damage.

In early September, when it became known that the last V1 had been launched from northern France, just ahead of the Allied advance, and Flak Regiment 155 (W) had retreated into the Netherlands, there was euphoria in London. Indeed, the Ministry of Information (MoI) authorised a press briefing, at which Duncan Sandys said, 'Except possibly for a few last shots, the Battle of London is over'. He then complimented the intelligence services, the active and passive defence forces, thanked the Americans for their wholehearted participation and the use of their equipment – and finally he praised the Londoners for bearing the price with great stoicism – but all this was a little premature. When one erudite reporter asked the crucial question, 'was there a rocket threat to come?' Sandys skilfully avoided a direct answer – and the champagne flowed in many a hierarchal circle that night. There was also talk of the Crossbow Committee standing down, despite wiser heads warning that, with a range of 200 miles, the V2 could reach London easily from elusive launch sites in the Netherlands, and that, if a longer-range version of the V1 was being developed, they too could rejoin the party. As evidence that the government knew this, Bomber Command was warned to prepare for a retaliatory, all-out gas attack against Germany, should a devastating V2 materialise.

The *Wehrmacht* launched their first V2s operationally on 8 September, Group North firing two at London from a site near The Hague, Holland, and Group South one against Paris from the Belgian town of St Vith, in the Ardennes. Learning from the past, the German launch crews were now mastering the art of camouflage and deception, maximising their ability to melt into the local environment to conceal themselves from the air, taking cover immediately any Allied air activity was suspected in their area and in any event as soon as they had fired their missiles, greatly enhancing their survivability. The Allies had few practical answers to this, one being to mount very expensive armed patrols over rocket-infested areas, in the hope of catching the enemy in the open, fleetingly, immediately before, during and after a launch, destroying them there and then. This was easier said than done, given the enormous area over which the fully mobile, transient V2 units moved. This could stretch from Scheveningen on the Dutch coast, across to the Rijsterbos in Friesland, then to Burgsteinfurt in Munsterland in Germany, down to Hachenburg, then west to Kottenforst, south-west of Bonn and on past Euskirchen to St Vith in Belgium, and up past Walcheren in Zeeland to the Hoek van Holland – but the area around The Hague remained the main hunting ground. There were reports of V2s being sighted as they rose from their launch pads, but some were suspect and only very rarely could successful attacks be carried out on the residual facilities which were slow to move. Neither radar, sound-ranging nor flash-spotting could do much to help find the rockets in such a wide area, and Bletchley was picking up very few tell-tale signals. Reliable information was rolling in from visual sightings by Belgian and Dutch resistance groups on the ground, pinpointing the rocket units and likely firing points, typically around the Rijksweg, Wassenaar and Duindigt districts of The Hague, and on Walcheren Island, but there could be no guarantee that these targets would still be visible, or even there, when bombers arrived; these were indeed fleeting targets.

CODENAME 'CROSSBOW'

On 17 September Bomber Command reacted immediately to a report by Dutch partisans on a V2 supply unit in a wooded area south-east of Wassenaar, by sending twenty-seven Lancasters and five Mosquitos to attack with twenty-four 250lb marker bombs and 169 tons of high explosives – but they were too late; the unit had either left or was never there – and nothing was achieved. On the same day twelve Spitfires of 229 Squadron from Coltishall, looking for launch sites close to the Dutch coastline, spotted a V2 streak away after launch, but they were too far away to find the exact location. Sometimes, however, the Allies were lucky. Acting on information that General Kammler was visiting Walcheren on 18 July, to witness the launch of the first V2 from there to London, RAF bombers carried out a successful attack on its supply lines, which resulted in the cancellation of the second round of firing scheduled that day. There was more evidence that attacks on V2 logistics targets were paying off when it became known, on 22 September, that Generals Kammler and Dornberger were concerned that the supply of liquid oxygen to the front line had been reduced to 200 cubic centimetres per day, enough to launch only twenty-four rockets a day.

Meanwhile, the burgeoning success of the V2 campaign in the autumn of 1944 was causing great concern in London, and specifically at Fighter Command HQ, Stanmore Park, where Air Marshal Sir Roderick Hill was primarily responsible for airborne countermeasures. With the agreement of his colleagues, the Chief of the Air Staff and Air Chief Marshal Sir Arthur Tedder, Eisenhower's deputy (Air) as Supreme Commander Allied Expeditionary Force, his fighter-bombers would attack any V2 target on sight, provided there was little or no danger to the local civilians. Also, his UK-based aircraft would, on a case-by-case basis, be authorised to pick up fuel at RAF airfields in liberated Europe, to enable them to carry out longer, more heavily-armed sweeps over rocket-infested areas. In November 2TAF fighter-bombers were cleared to do likewise and were blessed with early success against two trains moving to their launch areas carrying a total of forty V2s.

On 21 November, the latest CROSSBOW report from Duncan Sandys reflected the difficulties of finding and destroying rocket targets, *inter alia* admitting that the most important target of all, the massive Mittelwerk missile factory, some 300 feet below the Harz mountains, which was then producing thirty V2 a day, many V1s and other war assets, was all but invulnerable – even to the 12,000lb Tallboy seismic bombs. Also, it was now generally accepted that the transient Group North, located variously at Kleve and Burgsteinfurt on the Dutch/German border, had learned how best to operate relatively freely from the area surrounding The Hague, firing at London, while Group South, operating in the Euskirchen-Koblenz region, was doing likewise against targets in Belgium and France. On the table now was the unpalatable proposition of using heavy and medium bombers, at high and medium levels, albeit with their inherent inaccuracies, against rocket units buried in heavily populated areas around The Hague.

From the beginning of 1945 six Spitfire squadrons from Fighter Command acted as fighter-bombers against the elusive rocket launch sites in West Holland, and initially they enjoyed some success, but in February, when Flak Batteries 1/485 and 3/485 deployed to Duindigt, north of The Hague, the V2 launch rate increased. Almost in desperation it was suggested that AA on the east coast of England put up a screen of shrapnel into the expected path of an incoming rocket – but this idea was quickly rejected.

However, such was the clamour in London that the capital was having to bear too much of the pain that, at the end of January, the Defence Committee eventually agreed that the Haagse Bos, a wooded area, close to The Hague, which was thought to be hiding V2s, be attacked on 3 March, by a strong force of fifty-six 2TAF medium bombers. This ended in disaster, an error in the mission briefing or navigation resulting in the lead bombers dropping their bombs on the south-east of the woods, rather than the south-west, causing a fire storm in Bezuidenhout, a district overflowing with refugees from Wassenaar, which had been cleared by the Germans for their rocket operations. As a rough estimate, 500 civilians were killed, with 12,000 losing their homes and all their possessions. The tragedy seemed all the greater when it was found that the rockets said to be in the woods, had been moved out more than a week before. The inevitable court of enquiry blamed inadequate intelligence, mistakes by individuals and a failure of the staffs at 2TAF to learn from earlier sorties flown by Fighter Command. Those who had argued against this type of attack around The Hague had been right – and there would be no more raids of this kind in that area but fighter-bombers and armed reconnaissance aircraft would continue to play their deadly game of cat and mouse with the V2 rockets – a game neither player could win outright.

Then came another problem. Between midnight and 06.00 on 3 March launch crews of Flak Regiment 155 (W), deployed tactically in west Holland, fired thirty of its longer-range V1s at London, only two of which crossed the coast into England, and only one of these landing in Bermondsey, Greater London. Four days later RAF reconnaissance aircraft found two of the new launch sites, one on the airfield at Ypenburg and a second in a soap factory at Vlaardingen – relatively easy targets for the Spitfire fighter-bombers. On 8 March a platoon of Artillery Battery 3/485 fired its last V2s at London, one finding its mark on Smithfield Meat Market, with devastating results (Chapter Seven). In London John Mapplebeck reported that the sixty-five V2s hitting London that week showed a steady improvement in their accuracy – but it had all come too late.

The RAF fighter-bomber squadron commanders were now being given some discretion in the planning of their attacks, the charismatic commander of No.602 Squadron, Max Sutherland seizing the opportunity to do so when the Dutch Resistance reported that the Shell Mex Building in The Hague had become the HQ for the V2 operational staff, and his squadron was tasked with its destruction. He found that the width of the building, from his preferred direction of attack, equated to the wingspans of five of his Spitfire XVIs, line abreast, in which formation they would approach at rooftop height, with all cannon and machine guns blazing, to deliver their 250 and 500lb bombs, as they came within range. The risks were high, with intensive AA of all calibres to be expected at all points from landfall at Den Helder and thereafter as they departed over the Scheldt, but so were the potential rewards, and permission was given to proceed. No.453 Squadron from RAF Ludham would attempt to distract the enemy with a simultaneous attack nearby. The raid took place on 19 March 1945 and it went to plan with none of the aircraft lost. Max Sutherland's Spitfire did take hits as he pulled up rather imprudently to look back, with great satisfaction, at the Shell Mex building – now shrouded in smoke and dust, but he was able to limp on to their refuelling stop in Belgium. Among his pilots on that day was Flight Lieutenant Raymond Baxter, who would go on to become a prominent commentator and presenter for the BBC. 'Bax' remembers the moment that they roared over the roof of their target, at 400 mph, to be confronted, dead ahead, by a seemingly huge black cockerel, mounted on a weather vane on top of a church steeple, only his instinctive reaction saving the day by what must have seemed inches.

For the last eighteen months CROSSBOW operations had attempted, with only limited successes, to destroy or at least minimise the capability for the Wehrmacht to employ their flying bombs and rockets against the Allies. The manifold problems they faced have been well rehearsed above, and the costs were very high, not only in the diversion of air power from other wartime needs, but in military and civilian lives and material. There was, of course, no alternative but to use all possible means to protect the British homeland, a vital American stepping stone to the continent of Europe and launching point for the huge invasion forces poised to strike, and there could be no question of waiting for the final solution, that of occupying the missile sites. In February 1945 Hans Kammler, latterly in charge of all flying-bomb and rocket operations, gave some credit to the defenders, while noting the general impotence of Allied airpower:

> The counter-measures of the enemy increased considerably, especially as far as bombing and attacks by fighter-bombers were concerned ... . Supply lines were broken 44 times ... . This damage was remedied very quickly ... so that contrary to enemy air force statements reporting success, only negligible disturbance occurred, but never any definite stoppage in launching. From time to time it was necessary to stop operations during the day and launch only at night.

Perhaps the real truth lies somewhere between the two perceptions?

Chapter 9

Hochdruckpumpe – And What Next?

Before 1943 little was known about the third of Hitler's vengeance weapons, the *Hochdruckpumpe* (HDP), 'High Pressure Pump' - V3, but, had it become technically viable and operational earlier in the war, it could have added significantly to the Allies' problems, particularly with the impending invasion of France. The V3 was a massive super-gun, designed to fire high-explosive projectiles at London from a site close to the French coast. This multi-charge gun, to become known as 'The London Cannon', was the brainchild of August Coenders, a German artillery engineer working with the firm of Röchling-Stahlwerk AG. With an aerodynamic 'arrow-shell', Coenders sought to achieve an unprecedented muzzle velocity of 5,000 feet per second, or Mach 6, a speed which would give it a range of 100 statute miles, just enough to reach London. Made of chrome nickel steel, the 7-foot-9-inch finned projectile, weighing 310lb, and carrying an explosive charge of 55lb, was fired initially from the breech of 6-inch diameter and 490 feet long, smoothbore barrel. It was then accelerated up the barrel by a series of solid-fuel rocket booster charges, ignited electrically within each of sixteen pairs of diametrically-opposed lateral chambers, as the projectile passed up the central tube. Fins on the projectile imparted the necessary spin in flight, as rifling does for accuracy in the conventional shell or rifle bullet.

The first tests on the HDP, carried out in 1943 at the Hillersleben artillery range, Magdeburg, Germany, revealed problems in the projectile's design and the ignition of the rocket boosters, achieving muzzle velocities of only 3,300 feet per second – far below expectations. However, Albert Speer believed in the gun's potential and, having convinced Hitler that the project was worth pursuing, obtained his authority to carry out launch trials with a full-scale weapon at Misdroy on the Baltic island of Wolin. The re-designed projectiles, tested there between May and July 1943, increased the maximum range to fifty-eight miles before the gun destroyed itself – but still the trials continued. In March 1944 the HDP become the responsibility of the HWA, the Weapons Procurement Office, eventually joining the V1 and V2, under the control of Hans Kammler.

Meanwhile, the Führer had ordered the construction of two huge reinforced-concrete bunkers, deep underground in the limestone hill at Marquise-Mimoyecques, just south of Calais, and 103 miles from London. The two bunkers of Fortress Mimoyecques, codenamed *Wiese* (Meadow), were to be one kilometre apart, each to accommodate five batteries of five super guns, a total of fifty. They would be constructed by the German Todt Labour Organisation, employing German specialists, local French and Italian 'volunteers', all well separated domestically from the Soviet and Polish slave labourers, half of whom would not survive the project. Work on the site began in September 1943 and went on twenty-four hours a day, in two shifts, each of up to 1,500 men, initially to build the two tunnels, 100 feet below ground and 650 yards long, to serve a vast network of galleries and shafts, ultimately to be manned by a garrison of some 1,200 men from *Artillerie Abteilung 705*. In galleries 300 feet below the surface, the ammunition would be fed into the guns, which were all inclined at 50 degrees and pointed at London, protected on the surface by steel plates, 10-inches thick, laid on 16 feet of reinforced concrete. The target date for completion of the basic facility was December 1943, with the first cluster of five guns to be ready for action by March 1944, and twenty-five (half the planned total) by the following October.

Given that the visual clues to the existence of the bunkers were confined to twin rail lines vanishing into the Mimoyecques hills and a great deal of activity at the tunnel entrances, this might, at first, have generated only passing interest within an Allied intelligence community as it concentrated on the work in progress at the many V1 and V2 sites in the region. Indeed, it was not until 18 September 1943 that the photographic interpreters (PIs) at the CIU

Hochdruckpumpe on trial at Hillersleben Range, Magdeberg, Germany, 1943. (Courtesy Mimoyecques Museum)

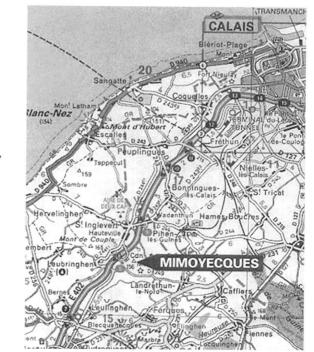

Right: The 'London Gun' lay deep underground in the limestone caves at Mimoychecques, south of Calais. (Author's Collection)

Below: Now the only entry/exit to the Mimoyecques underground museum. (Author, Courtesy Mimoyecques)

Above: The only way into Fortress Mimoyecques. (Author, Courtesy Mimoyecques)

Left: An early version of the *Hochdruckpumpe* in the underground museum at Mimoyesques, the booster chambers set here at 45 degrees, abandoned in favour of 90-degree settings. (Author, Courtesy Mimoyecques)

Five metres of reinforced concrete, topped by 20cm thick steel plates, protected the five muzzles of each HDP cluster. (Author, Courtesy Mimoyecques)

began to look more closely at the photos and, sensing something rather different, sounded the alarm. Sufficient evidence was then gathered, in short order, to justify two big CROSSBOW raids against the site.

On 5 November 1943 ('Fireworks Day' in Britain!) a huge force of No.2 Group Bostons and Mitchells was tasked against the excavations at Mimoyecques without revealing the nature of the target to the crews. Bad weather caused the Bostons to abort, but forty-eight Mitchells, using Gee, continued to France, where they were escorted by eighteen squadrons of Spitfires. As they approached the target they were greeted by heavy flak but no German fighters, and the first twenty-four Mitchells dropped 187 500lb HE bombs on the target, the second twenty-four missing the aiming point by 400 yards. As soon as it became clear that very little, if any, damage had been done to Fortress Mimoyecques, heavy raids were repeated on 8 and 9 November, using different tactics but again without achieving any significant damage.

Above and below: The seismic effects of 617 Squadron's 12,000lb 'Tallboy' bombs undermined the *Hochdruckpumpe*'s concrete structure, causing flooding below ground at Mimoyecques. (Courtesy Mimoyecques)

HOCHDRUCKPUMPE – AND WHAT NEXT?

Meanwhile, the Germans continued to have problems with the gun undergoing trials in Germany and it was these problems which probably explained why work on the second bunker was abandoned late in 1943 rather than any damage which might have been caused underground by the November raids. The London Cannon now consisted of only twenty-five guns, and a further reduction to fifteen installed in three banks of five, was ordered in the spring of 1944. The remaining site was raided again, twice in March, four times in April and three times in May 1944, causing peripheral damage above ground but again with no evidence that the work underground was affected. Following D Day on 6 June, attacks on Mimoyecques were stepped up, with three raids that month,

Wing Commander Leonard Cheshire led 617 Squadron's decisive raid on the HDP at Mimoyecques. (Courtesy Mimoyecques)

depositing 1,400 tons of high explosive bombs on the site, and when it seemed that the new weapon was about to become operational, two massive raids were planned for the 6 July. That morning, 100 Halifax heavy bombers delivered 464 × 2,000lb bombs, and in the afternoon sixteen Lancasters of the legendary 617 Squadron, led by Wing Commander Leonard Cheshire, each dropped a 12,000lb Tallboy bomb on the site, with great accuracy, leaving huge craters on the surface. What the Allies could not have known at that time, was that the seismic effects of the Tallboy explosions had led to the collapse of several arches at the 100-foot level, blocking the gun chambers and causing some flooding –with the result that the Germans decided to abandon Fortress Mimoyecques.

Given the problems being experienced during trials, the impending Allied occupation of the site, the air superiority over the Pas de Calais and reduced number of guns, the relatively small warheads and the possibility that the rounds might not even reach London, it was no surprise when the whole project was cancelled. Most of the labour force had departed by 26 July, leaving behind 120,000 cubic metres of redundant concrete. All things considered, the V3 was unlikely to have been more than another area 'terror weapon', probably less accurate than the V1 and V2 and certainly less destructive, while the cost, in men and material, was far too high when weighed against other imperatives at this crucial stage of the war. However, that was not the end of the story.

It seems that the Americans may not have heard, or been convinced, that the site had been evacuated, because a very special raid they had been planning on Mimoyecques went ahead anyway. Operation ANVIL was the US Navy (USN) equivalent of the USAAF's Operation APHRODITE, both top secret missions mounted from RAF Fersfield-Winfarthing airfield near Diss, Norfolk. These units were involved in what might be seen as a forerunner of today's precision guided munitions (PGMs), by exploring the concept of an unmanned 'drone', guided onto its target by radio control from a 'mother' aircraft, following behind. In these trial operations the drones would be redundant bombers, filled with high explosives, flown against high value, reinforced-concrete targets, such as submarine pens, command and control bunkers and weapons' silos, which were all but invulnerable to contemporary bombing. A pilot and an engineer were required to take off the USAAF B-17 and USN PBY4-1 drones manually and, when all was in order, hand over control to the mother aircraft, arm the explosives and bale out over a specified point in the UK. 'Mother', would be a Ventura medium bomber, flying slightly higher and 7 to 20 miles line astern, equipped with state-of-the-art radio control for *en route* and terminal guidance. The USAAF had flown several APHRODITE sorties already, without success, but the Mimoyecques ANVIL mission would to be the first to be carried out by the USN's Special Air Unit One, commanded by Commander James A. Smith.

Tasked to fly the heavily modified PB4Y-1 Liberator, No. 32271, on this special mission, were Lieutenants Joseph P. Kennedy Jr, the aircraft captain, and Wilford J. 'Bud' Willy, also a qualified Liberator pilot but on this day acting as co-pilot, radio control technician and weapons specialist. Joe Kennedy Jr, son of Joseph Patrick Kennedy Sr, the controversial US Ambassador to the UK at the beginning of the war, was being groomed unashamedly by his father to be the first Roman Catholic President of the USA. In 1942 Joe Junior put his law studies at Harvard on hold to become a naval aviator and, after graduating from flight school and completing his first tour on Mariner flying boats in Puerto Rico, came to England to fly

USN PB4Y Liberators on anti-submarine duties with Naval Squadron VB-110, operating from RAF Dunkeswell, in Devon. Despite having completed the required number of operational missions to render him eligible for a home posting early in 1944, he had applied to fly one sortie with Special Air Unit One, the ANVIL mission to Mimoyecques. He was then 29 years old. Bud Willy joined the USN in 1933, working his way up through the ranks to become a naval flier and Commander Smith's executive officer; he had 'pulled rank' on Kennedy's usual co-pilot, to fly this ANVIL trip. He was 35 years old.

The Liberator drone had been stripped of all non-essential equipment, with guns replaced by broom sticks in the hope of fooling any enemy intruder. It was loaded with 21,170lb of Torpex, in 374 boxes distributed securely throughout the aircraft, to be detonated by six Mk 9 demolition charges, each containing 100lb of TNT. After take-off from Fersfield, the drone and its entourage were to fly south-east to Framlingham, then north to Beccles, before turning south to Clacton, then to Dover and across the sea to the target. The two crewmen were to have baled out through a modified nose-wheel bay, near Manston, Kent, while the aircraft continued to be guided by 'mother' into the heavily-fortified tunnel entrances at Mimoyecques.

Kennedy took the heavy Liberator into the air at 17.59 on 12 August 1944 followed by two PV-1 Venturas (one as a reserve), two F-5 PR Lightning fighters, two B-17 Flying Fortresses for navigation assistance and to pick up the pilots, and a USAAF F-8 Mosquito photo aircraft, while P-51 Mustang fighters danced attendance around the group, ready to provide top cover. The formation then followed the planned route, turning left at Framlingham for Beccles, on which heading Kennedy began carrying out his final checks before handing over control to the Ventura, the codeword 'Spade Flush' also clearing Willy to switch on the TV camera in the Liberator's nose, to provide 'mother' with guidance to the target.

At 18.15 the tranquillity of the warm, cloudless evening over Suffolk gave way to an increasing rumble of aircraft approaching Darsham from the south, where 9-year-old Mick Muttitt was playing with his brother below the formation's flightpath. Mick was already an expert on aircraft operating in East Anglia but this cocktail of noise caused him to take a particular interest in this mixed group of aircraft, flying at a height he estimated to be 1,500 feet. He noted that the Liberator in the lead was trailing an ominous wisp of smoke from its bomb-bay and as the brothers watched, a mighty explosion rent the air, the aircraft disappearing in a fireball and re-emerging in a thousand pieces, the propellers of its engines still turning as they plunged to earth. Spellbound, Mick saw one Ventura pull high, while a F-5 or P-38 spun away to port as they took violent avoiding action. The Mosquito, having suffered some damage from the Liberator's debris, and with the photographer on board being slightly injured, made an emergency landing at nearby Halesworth. Mick recalls that the explosion left 'an enormous pall of black smoke resembling a huge octopus, its tentacles showing the earthward paths of burning fragments' and, in this inferno, both men aboard died. The time was 18.20.

There were no casualties on the ground, but up to 147 houses in the area were damaged, the wreckage being scattered across an area 3 miles long and 2 miles wide over Blythburgh Fen, starting many fires. At the scene on the following day Mick Muttitt found many fragments from the aircraft, a complete engine, part of a main undercarriage and tattered remnants of parachute – a poignant reminder of the two crewmen who had been aboard.

The Mimoyecques site was overrun by the Canadians on 5 September 1944 and a subsequent report recommended its 'complete destruction', allegedly to avoid the use of the residual facility by any future enemy and, on 9 May 1945, the Royal Engineers carried out Prime Minister Churchill's orders to do so. Part of the caves has now been re-opened and serves as a museum, a memory of the possible threat from the little known V3, and the enormous effort expended by the Allies to ensure it did not become operational; 1,375 Allied aircraft had dropped 6,517 bombs, with a total weight of 4,102 tons on Fortress Mimoyecques and many airmen had paid the ultimate price for attempting to do so. There were many reasons why the imaginative *Hochdruckpumpe* failed to materialise, but the effort expended on it serves again to illustrate the innovative spirit of the German scientists and technophiles in the 1930s and early 1940s when so many took advantage of rampant military ambitions to further their dreams, breaking new ground with

Lieutenant Joe Kennedy USN was killed when the PB4Y Liberator drone he was piloting towards Mimoyecques exploded in mid-air. (Author's Collection)

Right: Lieutenant 'Bud' Willy, Kennedy's co-pilot and weapons' specialist, also died on the Liberator bound for Mimoyecques. (Author's Collection)

Below: A PB4Y-1 Liberator was used by the US Navy for the ANVIL trials. (Author's Collection)

A USAAF Ventura bomber acted as 'mother' to guide the drone to its target. (Author's Collection)

One of the engines which spun to earth after the PB4Y exploded over Blythburgh Fen. (Derek Muttitt)

courage and determination. The V1, V2 and V3 are the best examples of this – but there were others.

The heroic action of Hanna Reitsch, in flying an Fi 103 flying bomb, modified with a cockpit and basic controls, to determine why so many had crashed immediately after take-off (Chapter Three), may have led to a desperate suggestion of suicidal flights by volunteer pilots in similarly modified V1s, to attack highly lucrative targets, primarily in London. Hitler agreed to the plan and there was no shortage of volunteers among the Luftwaffe's elite pilots to fly these 'one-way' missions. However, the Luftwaffe hierarchy would have none of it and persuaded Hitler to abandon the plan. V1s with cockpits remain to be seen in a few museums, one at la Coupole in the Pas de Calais, some carrying the misnomer 'V4' – the name more normally given to the *Rheinbote* (Chapter Five).

Several successors to the A4 rocket were considered, some reaching an advanced stage of design. The A5, A6, A7 and A8 variants were designated test vehicles but, in 1939, a larger and more powerful version of the A4 was tabled – with wings. One such test vehicle was given the name A4b, solely to secure priority in manpower and materials; this version had wings added to transfer the rocket's speed and altitude into aerodynamic lift, enabling the missile to glide as it descended into the denser air in the lower atmosphere, thereby significantly increasing its range, optimistically to 450 miles. When over the target the rocket would be sent into a near vertical dive, to give greater penetration and make airborne interception very difficult. Later, the wings were replaced by fuselage strakes, which increased the lift at supersonic speeds and eliminated the problem of transonic shift of the centre of lift. Such a rocket could be launched against the UK from deep inside Germany and it was this possibility which secured the blessing of Hitler in 1940. Following exhaustive tests in the Peenemünde wind tunnel, and a number of modifications, two A4bs were trialled at Blizna in December 1944; the first failed, but the second, a month later, was successful – until a wing fell off – after which, with time now running out for the rocketeers, the A4b trials were cancelled.

Aggregate 9 (A9) was intended to be used in conjunction with, and on top of a huge booster rocket, the A10, to target the United States, in *Projekt Amerika*. Work on the engine began in 1940 with Hermann Oberth and Walter Thiel (Chapter Two) coming together in 1941 with a plan to generate the required thrust of some 180 tons, employing a pack of six well-proven A4 engines. A special test rig was set up at Peenemünde, capable of measuring thrusts of up to 200 tons with expectations that this would propel the A9 at speeds of 2,700 mph up to altitudes of 245 miles. The A10 booster was re-designed in 1944, the six combustion chambers being replaced by a huge single chamber and expansion nozzle, burning diesel oil and nitric acid for 50 seconds to produce 1,670kN thrust. The target date for the first test flight was set for 1946 but, when it became clear that insufficient time remained to produce a suitable guidance system to take the rocket some 3,500 miles from Germany, this project too fell by the wayside. Nothing daunted, the team turned to an extraordinary alternative, in which a pilot would fly an A9 to the start of its terminal phase, assisted by radio beacons on U-boats and automatic weather stations strategically placed in the Atlantic. The author is unaware of any plans for the recovery of the pilot.

The A11 was even more ambitious, introducing a third, much larger, initial stage to boost a modified A10 and winged A9. The combination would be known as the *Japan Rakete*. Finally, the A12 was again based on experience with its immediate predecessors; it would provide the initial booster for heavily modified A11, A10 and A9 stages, for what would be a four-stage orbital rocket, expected to carry a payload of ten tonnes in a low earth orbit, but the war ended before either of these concepts could be pursued.

Although the two surface-to-air missiles (SAM), *Wasserfall* and *Enzian*, could not be classified as *Vergeltungswaffen* , they are worth a mention in being typical of several visionary projects which made use of developing technologies in the Aggregate rockets and their engines. Indeed, *Wasserfall* was a direct derivative of the V2 missile, albeit one quarter of the size, with an additional set of fins or 'air rudders' at the rocket's mid-point, and a warhead of 670lb. Dr Thiel also designed a different engine, to use a complex hypergolic liquid fuel, which could endure long periods of readiness on its launch pads. Initially, radio control by manual command line-of-sight (MCLOS) restricted the missiles use to daytime only and then only when the operator on the ground could maintain visual contact with his target, but later control would be radar-assisted. Conceived in 1941, the design was validated in 1942 and the hardware proven in 1943, the first successful flights taking place in 1944. Thirty five missiles were launched from Peenemünde before the site was evacuated in February 1945, but none were fired operationally.

Enzian was derived from the rocket-powered Messerschmitt Me163, which had failed as a fighter largely because of its limited duration of flight; a pilot-less missile, it was controlled from the ground by radio to explode a 1,100lb warhead ahead of a bomber stream in the hope of downing more than one of the formation as it flew into the fragmentation zone. Four *Schmidding* solid-fuel boosters produced a total of 15,000lb of thrust for a rocket assisted take-off (RATO), after which flight was sustained by a *Walther* liquid-fuelled engine (later replaced by a *Konrad* engine).The initial trials, which got underway in 1943, showed some promise, but also revealed difficult problems with the engine, proximity fuse and radio control. Messerschmitt persisted, but the well-developed *Enzian* had not become operational by January 1945 when all such projects were cancelled in order to concentrate every available resource on the Me262 fighter-bomber and the Heinkel He162 *Volksjäger* fighter.

The Nazis became aware of the potential of fusion and fission weapons in 1938, prompting a brief excursion into the nuclear world in April 1939 with the covert project *Uranprojekt* (Uranium Society). This ended shortly thereafter when Germany's invasion of Poland deprived the project of some of its key physicists when they were drafted into the *Wehrmacht*. Interest surfaced again in September 1939 when the HWA became involved in a three-pronged research programme concentrating on nuclear reactors, uranium isotope separation and heavy water production. This too had gained little momentum before it was decided, in January 1942, that atomic weapons could not become operational in Germany in time to have any impact on the war, and further exploration was handed over to the *Reichsforschungsrat* (Reich Research Council). The governing political hierarchy had failed to grasp the huge potential of nuclear weapons and such research programmes as continued with the few physicists who had not been diverted to higher

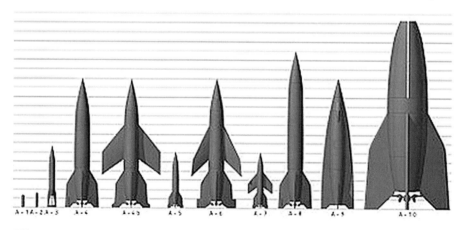

What Next? All these variants of the Aggregate rockets were being considered by the German visionaries of Peenemünde. (Author's Collection)

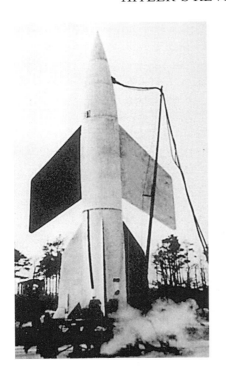

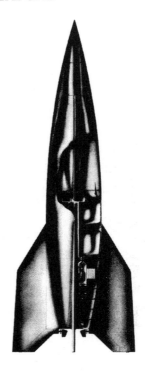

Above left: The Aggregate A4b had wings, and later fuselage strakes, to convert speed and height into lift, allowing the missile to glide to greater ranges in the lower atmosphere. (Author, Courtesy HTM Peenemünde)

Above right: The visionary A9 long-range rocket, with fuselage strakes. (Author's Collection)

Left: *Wasserfall* was a diminutive version of the A4 (V2), converted into a radio/radar-controlled surface-to-air missile (SAM); 35 test flights were flown before the project was abandoned in February 1945. (Author's Collection)

Enzian, an evolutionary SAM, used radio control and rocket technology based on the Me-163 fighter, but failed to reach operational status in the Second World War. (Author's Collection)

priority military tasks, limped on with no real progress made before the end of the war.

Thus ended a remarkable period of German innovation, improvisation and industry; had it been allowed to mature, history might have had a different story to tell.

Chapter 10

Hitler's Final Fling

On 16 December Operation *UNTERNEHMEN WACHT AM RHEIN* (WATCH ON THE RHINE), an unexpected German offensive involving 400,000 men, 1,200 tanks and 4,200 guns, caught a relatively weak force of American troops napping in the forests of the Ardennes. Making good use of landlines and with strict communications discipline, Allied intelligence had no specific information on the Germans' intentions in that area, the small number of hints detected 'on the wires' seemingly ignored. Moreover, very poor weather had kept Allied reconnaissance aircraft on the ground, so surprise was on the Germans' side. The *Wehrmacht*'s aim was to take back Antwerp, which had been occupied by the Allies since September, the port being crucial to them for reinforcement and re-supply, while at the same time encircling the Allied ground forces in the hope of then destroying them piecemeal.

As part of the plan V1s and V2s were fired at Antwerp from sites in Germany and Holland to 'soften up' the city. On 27 November 126 people were killed and 309 injured when a rocket hit close to the Central Station and, on the opening day of the offensive, another V2 demolished the Rex Cinema, causing the death of 567 Belgians and Allied troops, while injuring another 291 – the worst disaster to date in the history of the V-weapons. As a result, all the cinemas and theatres in the city were closed and large-scale gatherings prohibited.

Despite the difficult terrain favouring the defenders, and the pockets of fierce resistance, many German units made significant gains, benefitting from the surprise they had achieved and the poor weather which grounded Allied aircraft. However, any hopes of ultimate success were dashed on 23 December, when the weather cleared, allowing the might of the Allied air forces to be thrown against them, isolating many of their units, and denying them reinforcement and re-supply, with the result that the Germans were stopped short of the River Meuse.

The turbulence caused by the Ardennes campaign, and the almost continuous bombardment of Antwerp by the V1s and V2s, severely hampered the movement of supplies from its docks and the problem was exacerbated by the lack of transport, especially rolling stock, when freight cars were withdrawn to prepare for a possible evacuation of Liège and Luxembourg City, on which the German forces were advancing. After this scare, the output from the port increased, thanks in part to an American initiative with their 'ABC Haul', a system plying between Antwerp, Brussels and Charleroi involving some sixteen haulage companies using 5-ton tractors hauling 10-ton trailers – but this would not prove enough.

The failure of the Ardennes offensive brought much relief to the Allied camp but on New Year's Eve the Germans struck again with Operation *BODENPLATTE* (BASEPLATE), a series of massive air attacks by the Luftwaffe on the Allies' airfields in France, Belgium and Holland. *BODENPLATTE* should have been timed to support the leading panzers, which had been expected to cross the Meuse in late December, well on their way to Antwerp, but with the armour failing to reach the river, the aim of the operation was changed to that of causing maximum degradation of Allied air power when it was likely to be most vulnerable – early on New Year's Day. So it was then that 1,000 German fighters and fighter-bombers, from eleven Luftwaffe wings, converged on seventeen Allied airfields, at low level to avoid radar, to attack with bombs, rockets and gunfire on their unsuspecting and perhaps rather drowsy victims. Three hundred Allied aircraft were destroyed on the ground, a further 146 seriously damaged and another seventy were lost in the air, split almost evenly between the RAF and the USAAF. However, the Allied fighter pilots and gunners had responded well, contributing to the destruction of 300 of the attacking aircraft, albeit with a number of these downed by over-zealous AA gunners back at the German bases. The reason for committing this huge slice of what remained of the Luftwaffe, when it was so badly needed to protect the Reich itself, and to support the German Operation *WIRBELWIND* (WHIRLWIND), against a rapid advance by the US Seventh Army, was hard to understand. Was it to help protect their ground forces from Allied air attacks as they retreated back through the Ardennes, or simply to reduce the Allied capability to seek and destroy their V1 and V2 launch sites in Holland and west Germany?

Given that the V1's accuracy increased as ranges decreased , the Germans had set up three new launch sites in the Rotterdam area, a mere fifty-six miles from Antwerp, giving them a better chance of hitting point targets in the port – and so the results proved. The new sites were ready for action, with 300 bombs, by the end of January; they were artfully concealed within high buildings, one a port warehouse, another a sugar factory, and the fact that the bombs were only revealed when the doors of a building opened to fire them, posed new problems for the defenders. *Inter alia,* the Allies now had to re-deploy their AA defences astride new lines of attack from Rotterdam in the north.

BODENPLATTE had certainly been a timely wake-up call for the Allies, signalling that Germany could still spring surprises; their aircraft losses could not be made good overnight and an immediate review of active and passive defence measures at Allied air bases was undertaken. Standing air patrols were considered but this very expensive option, which also required the re-assignment of assets intended to support Allied ground forces advancing into Germany, was rejected, except in specific circumstances, in favour of higher readiness states. The air defence of Antwerp had lapsed temporarily when many of the gunners had to re-role as infantry to face a possible attack by German ground troops from the Ardennes, but they were soon able to revert to their AA duties. They now faced V1 attacks from the north and the east and a continuing problem for the defenders was the co-ordination of AA with Allied aircraft using a major airfield north of Antwerp, which lay beneath the flight path of new missile streams.

Offensive action against V1 and V2 targets on the ground was also proving increasingly difficult, as the Germans continued to improve their movement control, camouflage and deception, and as new missile sites were developed to threaten Antwerp and Liège. The RAF's Second Tactical Air Force had, alone, flown 10,000 sorties against missile connected targets in the three months September-November 1944 and, despite the distraction of the Ardennes offensive and *BODENPLATTE,* there was no intention of letting up on this campaign. In this, the Americans were playing a full part, adding more P-51 Mustangs of the US 8th Air Force to this game of 'hide and seek' – but to the detriment of their primary purpose, that of escorting their heavy bomber force.

Continuing into 1945 the heavy V1 and V2 raids on the port of Antwerp were now having a critical effect on the unloading of men and supplies, with an alarming number of both missiles falling onto or close to the cargo ships. On 8 January the freighter *Blenheim* was put out of commission for a month, and the *Michael De Kovats* was seriously damaged a week later. The ship discharge rate was far less than had been expected and future targets had to be lowered to 496,000 tons in January, 504,000 tons in February and 551,000 tons in March. The citizens of Antwerp were also suffering badly; with their city being only a few feet above sea level, they had no deep shelters to protect them, such as were available to the Londoners. Moreover, many Belgian labourers refused to work in the primary target areas and had to be seduced back to their jobs with additional pay, which in turn caused much resentment among those who continued to do their duty on the fringes, where they were by no means safe from the bombs.

The many problems caused by this continuous assault on Antwerp combined to persuade the authorities to recommend that ammunition ships be denied entry to the port, on the grounds that if they took a hit from either of the V-weapons much of the port could be destroyed. The Allied naval command felt that this total embargo was unacceptable but agreed to a compromise that only ammunition and explosives needed urgently for operations, typically for AA units defending the port, should be landed in Antwerp, and then only in a remote part of the port where special precautions could be enforced. In fact, throughout the whole period of the V1 and V2 attacks, very few dangerous cargos were brought ashore in Antwerp, the vast majority having to travel the 500 miles from Cherbourg or 275 miles from le Havre to the front line, causing congestion on the roads and massive delays – while using many hundreds of gallons of precious motor fuel. All this affected the work rate, and prompted the search for an additional port.

Even before the flying bomb and rocket attacks had begun, the Americans had questioned the Allies' reliance on the port of Antwerp and now, with additional restrictions on its use by explosives and ammunition carriers, plans were dusted off for the joint use by the British and the Americans of Ghent as a back-up gateway for reinforcements and supplies into the continent. The situation there was far from ideal, extensive dredging being necessary before the waterways could be used by deep-water oceangoing ships while many of the port facilities needed repair – but on 23 January the first of many cargo ships, the Liberty ship *Hannis Taylor* entered the port. Given the problems at Antwerp, where even the revised targets might not be met, the port facilities at Ghent were greatly welcomed.

In January 1945 Himmler brought the rocketeers and the flying-bomb men together in an *Armeekorps zur Vergeltung* (Army Corps for Retaliation, or 'Revenge Corps'), commanded by Hans Kammler, with *Oberst* Georg Thom as his deputy. Also under the new command was the first (and only) *Rheinbote* battery (*Artillerie 709*), based at Nunspeet in Holland, which began its own bombardment of Antwerp on Christmas Eve 1944 and by mid-January, had reported forty-five successful firings. In fact, *Rheinbote* did little or nothing to help disrupt activities in the port. The projectiles had relatively small warheads, they were likely to have been spread over a wide area and it was believed that many overshot their aiming point. No records can be found of where the missiles fell, and in the absence of any definitive evidence of its success, Kammler cancelled the *Rheinbote* programme on 6 February, the missile having already consumed significant resources in manpower and material, to no good purpose.

At the same time, Dr Waldemar Peterson, who headed the commission to oversee Germany's long-range bombardment operations, had a stroke, creating a vacancy at the helm. Dornberger, having recently been passed over as head of his V2 programme, was offered this unenviable role but declined, considering that the problems he would face would be nigh insoluble. This shock rejection threw the missile hierarchy into confusion, and brought von Braun in as arbiter. Von Braun suggested that the bureaucratic commission be disbanded, and that Dornberger be invited to head a group of dedicated scientists and engineers to pave the way ahead for the missile, and with full agreement *Arbeitsstab Dornberger* (Working Staff Dornberger) was formed on 12 January 1945 as part of the development department of the ministry of munitions.

Priorities in the operational commitment of the V1 continued to be controversial. Wechtel championed their use as 'terror weapons', specifically targeting London, while other military commanders demanded their use against targets which would affect the battle raging across Europe, examples being Antwerp and Liège. Also, there was increasing concern over the number of German soldiers and civilians killed and injured when errant missiles fell among them, 124 of them having crashed within central Holland in one twelve-day period in January. The missilemen seemed unable to solve the problem; could it be down to human error among the very busy, tired and war-weary launch crews? The launch units were also being deprived of the fuel they needed to sustain the bombardment ordered, less than half the requirement being delivered to them in January, while the bombs issued to them fell from 160 to 100.

Himmler's man Hans Kammler was in the ascendancy again. In January he was promoted to *SS Obergruppenführer*, no longer subordinate to Speer, and given command of the Revenge Corps, with control over both V1 and V2 programmes. He immediately expanded and re-organised the forces under his command and set his sights on embracing *Arbeitsstab Dornberger*. Wechtel's units, now combined within 5 Flak Division (W) remained in the Luftwaffe, and went about their business as usual, with orders to prepare for further attacks on London from launch sites in Holland, with the longer-range V1s undergoing final flight trials. However, when his officers were ordered to join the *Waffen-SS*, some, including *Oberst* Eugen Walter, acting commander of the division, refused, and was ordered to step aside, to be replaced in February by Max Wechtel. To consolidate his power, Kammler persuaded Göring to appoint him 'Special Commissioner for Breaking the Air Terror', making him the most powerful man in the Third Reich outside the ruling circle of the Nazi Party.

V1 and V2 launch crews were now overcoming many of the teething and quality control problems with their respective weapons, the failure rate of the latter decreasing from 37 per cent to 12 per cent by the end of 1944. Frustratingly, although the V2 units were under continuous surveillance and strafing, which kept them on the move, their firing rates remained high. On 26 January one regiment launched seventeen rockets successfully against England, and Antwerp continued to suffer greatly from an average of ninety-eight bombs per week, with a peak on one day of 160, while the bombs fired over the shorter distance from Rotterdam to Antwerp proved to be 25 per cent more accurate than those launched from farther afield.

Back at Peenemünde the engineers were struggling with a major programme of modifications to the V2 to increase its range, improve guidance and simplify production, but now with a much reduced workforce. Those who remained on Usedom were painfully aware of the steady advance of the Red Army towards them and the retribution which would surely be meted out to them following the atrocities committed by German soldiers on the Russian front in 1941. They were already suffering from severe shortages of all things and some of the inhabitants were thinking of defecting to the West, to surrender to the Americans or British rather than the Russians, but the commander, General Rossmann, would have none of it, ordering everyone to remain at their posts and threatening dire retribution for any who transgressed. All able-bodied men between the ages of 16 and 60 were ordered to join the *Volksstrum* (Home Guard). However, on 31 January 1945, Kammler ordered that the work in progress at Peenemünde be re-located to the south and to the west, together with 4,325 workers, using every available means of transport, including horses, carts and river barges, while each manager searched for temporary sanctuaries where they could continue their work. No provision was made for the workers' families or dependants.

Werner von Braun arranged for the main party to move to Bleicherode, west of Nordhausen, where a centralised engineering co-operative *Entwicklungsgemeinschaft Mittelbau*, which embraced a number of other military industries, was allegedly being set up and where he aimed to continue his work on the rockets, but *en route* to Bleicherode, he and his driver fell asleep, von Braun breaking his arm badly in the crash which followed. What they found at Bleicherode was far from encouraging; much of their equipment had been lost in transit and few preparations had been made for their arrival. Hermann's all-important supersonic wind tunnel went to Bavaria while another team, led by Dr Kurt Debus, the chief of Test Stand VII, went west to 'Fortress Cuxhaven', in the hope of continuing flight trials from there. Joining them was the Luftwaffe's V1 team from *Flakgruppe Zempin* and *Peenemünde West*. Meanwhile, Bletchley noticed that, one by one, the many signals cells once involved with the missiles along the Baltic coast were ceasing transmissions. Close to Bleicherode, Mittelwerk was continuing to produce V1s and V2s, but in progressively more chaotic conditions. In the chaos, Russian PoWs broke out of captivity and killed their guards, but their freedom was shortlived; they were hunted down and executed, together with others in their bunker, their bodies left hanging outside the entrances to the tunnels to discourage others.

Proof that a new lightweight version of the V1 was in the offing came when one which landed near Antwerp without exploding was found to have a wooden nose, this giving the clue that they might have the range to reach London from sites in Holland and presaging a new assault on the capital. The new, long-range version of the V1 did become available in March, with the flight time increased from 30 minutes to 43 minutes, more than enough to reach England from well inside Holland, but at the expense of the warhead which was reduced from 1,830 to 1,169lb of high explosives. Thus Wachtel's men resumed their offensive against London on 3 March, firing a total of thirteen V1s from midnight to 06.00, but only two of these crossed the coast into England, and only one reached London – landing at Bermondsey.

With the winter weather succumbing to spring, Allied PR aircraft had begun to enjoy more success and on 26 February alone they had found three V1 sites. An immediate attack on one, by rocket-firing Typhoons, was inconclusive, the clever selection of the site making its destruction difficult and it recovered quickly, to fire seven missiles against London that night. In the second week of March the new V1s were launched against London from Vlaardingen, Ypenburg and Delft, in Holland, the bombardment continuing thereafter, with 116 of the missiles fired against London by 20 March – although many of these fell to newly-deployed fighters and AA. To meet this new threat, multiple gun arrays straddled the new approach lanes to be expected, together with a force of six squadrons of P-51 Mustangs and three squadrons of Meteor jets, held at high states of readiness by day, while two squadrons of Mosquitos and one of Tempests stood guard at night. Learning from the past, the fighters were well separated from the GDAs.

Back at Antwerp the ABC fleet continued its sterling work, transporting 245,000 tons of supplies to the battle front from 30 November to 26 March but continuous missile attacks, coupled with random attacks by the Luftwaffe on the road and rail network, were still having a very detrimental effect on activities in the port. A total of 1,712 V2s had struck Greater Antwerp and the west side of the Scheldt River, 152 hitting the docks, killing fifty-three soldiers and 131 civilians, while a further thirty-one rockets fell on the outskirts. Extensive damage in the docks included two warehouses, twenty berths, a canal lock, a 150 ton crane and 150 ships either sunk or damaged, while much time was wasted when the stevedores had to take shelter from the bombs or be diverted to repair work – many also suffering from continuous 'nervous strain'.

With a dearth of German heavy artillery to lay siege to the huge Allied supply centre at Liège, Wachtel's flying bombs were called on to do the job, beginning on 20 November and taking everyone there by surprise. Throughout the next ten days the residents, transient and permanent, suffered the alarming effects of 331 V1s until the first phase of the offensive ceased on 30 November. There was then a pause before the start of the second phase on 15 December which coincided with the German offensive in the Ardennes, Luftwaffe bombers and fighter-bombers joining in (when the weather allowed) a continuous bombardment of Liège, with the railyards in this vital communications centre the primary target. This phase continued until March, by which time more than a thousand V1s had struck Liege and in its immediate vicinity, killing ninety-two Allied soldiers and wounding 336. The civilian population fared even worse, with a total of 1,158 casualties, massive disruption to the local infrastructure and 97 per cent of its 82,700 dwellings destroyed or damaged. Perhaps the Germans were not aware of the death and destruction they had wrought on Antwerp and Liège, no longer having sufficient PR aircraft or an effective intelligence network to make valid assessments.

With the V2s continuing to present ever greater problems in England and on mainland Europe and with the fighter-bomber attacks on sites around The Hague having little success, Home Secretary Herbert Morrison raised again the need for more intensive bombing of the V2 sites, if necessary with less precision using medium and heavy bombers. Controversially, it was argued that the Dutch must bear a share of the onslaught being suffered by Londoners. However, fearing excessive collateral damage on a friendly country, the Defence Committee found against an all-out bombardment by 'the heavies', only agreeing, with reservations, to the limited use of the generally more accurate medium bombers of 2TAF against selected targets. Perhaps there was little heed to the 'law of unintended consequences'? So it was that, on 3 March 1945, fifty-six medium bombers were sent to saturate the Haagsche Bos, a small, heavily wooded area from which many launches were known to have come, to deliver sixty-nine tons of bombs from 12,000 feet. However, success depended on up-to-date intelligence and, with the target being in the middle of a highly populated area, the very best of precision bombing. In the event, the enemy had already departed from the Haagsche Bos and the bombs fell well wide of the original aiming point – at enormous cost to the Dutch residents of Bezuidenhout (See Chapter Eight).

On 23 March the Allied armies were on the verge of crossing the Rhine in strength and elements of Kammler's Revenge Corps were ordered to retreat east, with as much of its equipment (including rockets) as possible, and to continue firing on London from any new sites they could find. Together with the units around The Hague, the V2 bombardment of London continued, with destructive strikes on Tottenham Court Road, Stepney (twice), Edmonton, Cheshunt, Ilford, Hutton and Orpington. With desperation in the air, the Germans tried hard to destroy the key bridge over the river Rhine

Rural, wooded areas on the west coast of Holland were used extensively for launching V2s against England in late 1944 and early 1945, leaving craters such as these along this track in Bergen Op Zoom. (Medmenham Collection)

Above and below: Last Gasp. In the last months of the Second World War *Flak Abteilung 444* fired a final 77 V2s against England from the small forest of Het Rijsterbos, in Friesland, Holland. The author's wife, a child living there at that time, reads the history at the forest entrance. (Author)

With natural and man-made camouflage readily available in West Holland, it was rare to find V2s in the open, ready to launch, these two PR shots, taken on 26 Feb 1945, merely revealing post-launch craters in the Duindigt area of Wassenaar, close to The Hague. (Medmenham Collection)

at Remagen after it had been captured by the Americans on 7 March. Firing eleven V2s, surely more in hope than expectation for this point target, caused a great deal of collateral damage and fatalities among the American forces nearby – but the bridge survived.

Kammler's men were now very tired; they were facing endless disasters on the battle front, very heavy workloads and ever-changing plans, having to travel long distances, only at night, to attend endless meetings. However, he himself seemed tireless and had no patience with those who could not keep up with him – often using a burst of his tommy-gun to wake them from their slumbers. Production of the V-weapons continued apace, with streams of railcars carrying them from Mittelwerk to the front, but as the railways came under ever increasing attacks from the Allied bombers and the Dutch Resistance, so more soldiers were needed to guard them.

So it was that the last V2 was fired at London, by Battery 1/485 at The Hague, at 16.48 on 27 March 1945, landing in Orpington, Kent, 15 miles from its aiming point, killing one and injuring twenty-three. One day later, at 08.49, Battery 2/485 fired its last V2 at Antwerp, from Burgsteinfurt, Germany, the rocket landing 11 miles north-east of its target, at Ossendrecht. The V2 units then simply melted into Germany, to destinations largely unnoticed in the confusion of the time. The last V1 to be launched against London, from Delft in Holland, landed at Datchworth, Herts, at 16.00 on 29 March while two others which followed were brought down by AA, one at Sittingbourne, Kent, the other off the coast at Orfordness. Shortly thereafter, Mr Churchill announced that the missile attacks on England were over. Antwerp had to suffer from the V1s until 30 March – after which the missilemen were in full retreat, some re-roling, with great reluctance, as infantry soldiers. Although there had been plans to use the V-weapons against the Russians, these did not materialise.

In the last week of March Bletchley Park decoded a message from the Revenge Corps, which hinted strongly that its rocketmen were about to evacuate West Holland, and this was ordered by Kammler in a signal on 31 March; their fate was also to become infantry soldiers, in a final attempt to repel the Russians on the river Weser, north of Hannover. This was indeed a dismal prospect for them, given that, of the 1,000 gunners who had been sent as infantrymen to the Russian front in January, only 100 had returned in March, to the rallying point at Suttrop, in north Sauerland. Suttrop was also the scene of one of Kammler's most brutal executions when he ordered *Obersturmführer* Wolfgang Wetzling to exterminate 208 slave labourers who were found cooking chickens in the surrounding woods as they tried to walk home to Russia.

Amongst all this chaos, missile production at Mittelwerk continued with 617 V2s and 2,275 V1s assembled there in February while plenty of components and the necessary machinery remained to manufacture more. Earlier plans to fire-bomb the tunnel entrances to the underground works had been shelved, but the RAF did bomb Nordhausen on 2/3 April, virtually destroying the old city and killing an estimated 8,000 people, including some 1,500 prisoners in the Boelcke Luftwaffe barracks. The Americans arrived there shortly thereafter, to find that many of the starving and dying prisoners of Camp Dora had been murdered by the guards, in one case 1,000 having been herded into a building and burned to death. SS guards then packed trains with an estimated 4,000 prisoners from Mittelwerk for transport to Bergen-Belsen Concentration Camp in Lower Saxony ready to resume work on the missiles there once the Germans had prevailed over the Allies. This route took them north via Gardelegen where their journey ended six days later, the rail lines beyond having been destroyed by Allied bombs. Those prisoners who had not died already were then herded into a barn full of straw soaked in petrol and burned to death, many of those trying to escape being gunned down by the guards, most of whom then defected and melted into the countryside. Much of the production and supporting equipment at Mittelwerk was then destroyed as the *Wehrmacht* retreated, but there were still many spoils of war to be had when the Allies arrived (Chapter Eleven).

On 1 April Kammler ordered 500 people, including von Braun, to leave Bleicherode – again without their families – to an unspecified destination 'where you can continue your important work'. Those remaining at Bleicherode were simply left to face the Russians. The 'Vengeance Express', which had been home to many of the top rocketeers since their days in Blizna, rolled out of Bleicherode on 6 April, for the six-day journey to the Bavarian Alps. Von Braun realised that further work would not be practicable without all the notes and equipment left behind or lost *en route* and knew, realistically, that they were simply fleeing for their lives. He ordered his assistant, Dieter Huxel, to collect all the classified documents he could lay his hands on and take them, in three large trucks, to a hiding place in a mineshaft near the town of Dörnten, north of the Harz mountains, from where they could be retrieved at a later date, leaving him to make his own way south to Oberammergau. There, von Braun, Dornberger and others were accommodated at a hotel in the ski resort of Oberjoch, on the Austrian-German border, waiting to surrender to Americans. Von Braun was now suffering severely from incorrect treatment to his broken arm, but a local ski surgeon put this right by breaking the plaster cast and resetting the bone before confining him to bed. In the weeks to follow, the many photographs taken of him as a prisoner of the Americans, would show his arm raised as if in a salute – but not to the Führer!

Kammler seems to have departed from the Revenge Division on 7 April, and was later believed to have attempted to muster a few remaining troops for a futile fight against the Americans before he himself escaped to Prague, where it is said he shot himself to avoid capture by Czech partisans. On 14 April the Revenge Division was ordered to re-role as infantry, to face the oncoming Russians on the river Elbe but, in Kammler's absence, the divisional commanders thought better of it and, on 26 April, they surrendered to the US Army, hoping that their proven knowledge of missile operations would stand them in good stead in what followed. They were disarmed on the Elbe and taken into captivity, only too pleased to escape the Russians – who failed in their demands that they should be their prisoners.

Hostilities in Europe ceased on 8 May 1945.

Chapter 11

The Spoils of War and Operation Backfire

Forward thinkers, particularly among the three great Second World War Allies, the Americans, Russians and British, undeniably impressed by the German innovation which resulted in the *Vergeltungswaffen*, were now anxious to lay their hands on their definitive designs, hardware and expertise – and the Russians were the first to do so when they occupied Blizna on 6 August 1944.

In a letter to Stalin, dated 13 July 1944, Churchill alerted the Russians to the importance of the missile testing range at Blizna when he sought his permission for a group of British specialists to visit the area once it had been occupied by Soviet troops. Stalin agreed but, having been so alerted, he ordered Major General P.I. Fedorov, director of NII-1 (Russian Research Institute) to pre-empt the British visit by taking his own team to scour the area in early August, and remove anything which might be of value to their own research. In fact, it was soldiers of General Kurochkin's Sixtieth Soviet Army who recovered the first pieces of the V2 found there in the second week of August, before the NII-1 team arrived. At that time the Russians had little knowledge of rocket technology nor any idea what they were looking for because when the British arrived, armed with maps of the launch areas and other points of interest on the range, together with details of the missiles, they found many useful remnants to take back to London for evaluation.

At the end of the war, the Soviets were in control of 600 German aircraft plants, or 50 per cent of the total capacity, but they wanted more as reparations for the damage the Germans had done to their country. Clearly the defeated country could not pay the millions of dollars demanded, so Joseph Stalin set up a 'Trophy Committee', consisting of representatives of Soviet industries, tasked with seeking out and securing anything of potential scientific or technological value and shipping them back to

Russia, as their armies marched into Germany, rocket science being high on their list of priorities.

The next source of interest was Peenemünde where the Germans had stripped down every facility and strived to destroy anything of value on missile hardware and documents, but the Russian NII-1 specialists still found much of interest when they arrived there on 2 May 1945. They discovered large items from various Aggregate rockets, launching platforms and a complete *Rheinbote* rocket gun, in addition to many documents on other projects, including a revolutionary rocket-propelled aircraft which undoubtedly helped the Russians with this new science. Most of the German scientists and senior specialists had already fled south but the Russians did capture Helmut Gröttrup, one of von Braun's chief assistants and initially 200 of Gröttrup's colleagues, from which nucleus grew a body of some 5,000 workers from all skill levels which was put to work repairing and salvaging what they could to return Peenemünde to a productive unit – albeit as a shadow of its former self. What might have seemed like a good deal to the Germans, for them to have a job at all in their war-torn country, let alone one with which many of them were already acquainted, came to an abrupt end a year later. On 22 October 1946 Stalin ordered Operation

A British soldier inspects a V2 and its Mielerwagen transporter/erector at a typical forest launch site somewhere in Holland. (Medmenham Collection)

American troops discovered 'ready to use' V2s on railway wagons close to the Mittelwerk production centre. (Medmenham Collection)

OSOAVIAKHIM, the removal and dispersal of the whole facility and many of the workers, ostensibly on five-year contracts, to separate sites in Russia, where work would continue on weapons development. Gröttrup himself was working under the eminent Russian rocket engineer Sergei Korolev in NII-88 on Gorodomiya Island. At the same time some Russian scientists were sent to Germany to study at appropriate academic institutions, while back-engineering and a new fuel produced a successful Russian version of the A4 (V2), the R-11; this rocket, which emerged in 1955, had a range of 170 statute miles. The German workforce, effectively kidnapped in 1946, would remain in Russia for several years, helping to breathe new life into Russian advanced weapons technology, until they were no longer needed when they were returned to Germany.

It was, however, the Americans who won the 'jewel in the crown' of Germany's missile legacy when they arrived at Nordhausen and its massive weapons factory, underground at Mittelwerk, on the southern edge of the Harz mountains. This prize fell to Combat Command B (CCB) of 3rd Armored Division, US Army, which discovered the horrors within the tunnels of Mittelwerk and at Camp Dora but also a treasure trove of complete missiles, missile components and ancillary equipment, much of it loaded on freight trains ready to leave for the front. Wasting no time the US Chief of

Army Ordnance Technical Intelligence in Paris, Colonel Holgar Toftoy, sent teams of experts to Mittelwerk to raid the offices and workshops for every technical detail on the two missiles, and initiated 'Special Mission V2', the evacuation of 100 V2s and associated equipment to the USA.

With commendable dispatch, and paying little heed to an earlier agreement that any such find would be split equally between the Americans and British, the first forty of 341 fully loaded railway wagons left Mittelwerk for Antwerp docks on 22 May, the last leaving on 31 May. Within days, the first of sixteen Liberty ships left Antwerp for New Orleans, to be trucked on to White Sands Proving Ground, New Mexico. The CCB may have been unaware then that Mittelwerk would be in the Soviet zone of occupation because a residue of missile equipment remained there for the Russians to find when they arrived on 21 June.

There remained the need for experienced German missilemen to clarify the technical details needed to avoid the problems found during the testing, trials and launching of the missiles at Peenemünde, Blizna and elsewhere, and in helping to 'reverse-engineer' the missiles, and it was down to Major Robert Staver of the US Ordnance Office to find this expertise. The big fish, including von Braun, had by this time surrendered to the Americans in the lower Baverian Alps, and were under guard in Garmisch Partenkirchen where selection for employment on rocket work in America was taking place. However, back at Nordhausen, Staver found V2 engineer Otto Fleisher and structural engineer Walther Riedel who were only too pleased to help, again with the prospect of emigration to the United States. A further search of the area revealed another pool of expertise, covering most aspects of missile technology, from which von Braun's engineers identified the men they thought would be of most use to the Allies and, on 20 June 1945, the best of these were moved a few miles south-west, to Witzenhausen, in the US Zone, one day before the Russian occupation of Nordhausen. Angered that the Americans had taken the best of the missile bounty, and having failed to woo more than a handful of potentially useful German scientists and technicians into their employ, the Russians hatched a plan to kidnap some or all of those now lodged temporarily at Witzenhausen. They entered the town with convincing paperwork and dressed in British military uniforms (believing they were in the British Zone) but the American guards were smart enough to detect the ruse and sent them on their way.

There only remained that huge cache of documentation on the *Vergeltungswaffen*, so scrupulously recorded in the German way and hidden by Dieter Hexel in the old mine at Dörnten, to give the Americans all they wanted to pursue rocket technology in the their own backyard (Chapter Ten).

Again Staver came to the rescue when he found one of the few remaining missilemen at Nordhausen, Karl Fleisher, who knew where the documents were hidden and, on 20 May 1945, he led the Americans to them.

The Americans may have secured the lion's share of the rich pickings to be had at Mittelwerk, but a Soviet 'Special Purpose Brigade' still managed to find some items of interest which were assembled in Berka, near Zonderhausen, run by Major General Tveretsky and veterans of the Russian *Katyusha* (Rocket) units. Further missile 'trophies' found in Bad Sachsa, a stopping-off place for the Peenemünde party heading south, were said to have been shared with the Americans. Meanwhile, a key member of NII-1, Boris Chertok, who was already making use of the missile expertise of German specialists found languishing in Russian prison camps, arrived at Nordhausen as late as July 1946 and still managed to make contact with, and recruit, the few German missile technicians still there. Finally, the Russians also lured a few more of the German rocketeers from the care of the Americans in Bavaria with better pay and food, and the chance to stay in Germany, but all these efforts paled into insignificance compared with the Americans' rich pickings.

The British, having been outwitted by the Americans on the '50:50 per cent' deal, did their best to make up ground with a Special Projectile Operations Group (SPOG). While they already knew much about the rocket from the errant V2 which had crashed in Sweden and from good intelligence work by Polish and Dutch partisans (Chapter Four), they needed to know more, particularly on the operational missiles' support equipment. This being so, and with so many rocket scientists and 8,000 German rocket troops now in Allied hands to help them, the British secured permission from Supreme Commander Eisenhower to 'to ascertain the technique for launching long-range rockets, and to prove it by actual launches'. SPOG was tasked with demonstrating the preparations for – and firing of – three fully serviceable V2s into the North Sea, monitored by radar, from a well-equipped German naval gun range at Altenwalde, south of Cuxhaven. The War Office was given ultimate responsibility for Operation BACKFIRE, with Major General Cameron in command and Colonel W.S. Carter running the demonstration; the Americans would provide support and the exercise would be witnessed by a selected audience from the Allied Powers. Wernher von Braun and Gen Dornberger were released from American custody, temporarily, to advise the British, particularly on matters of safety and security, propellant storage, transport, loading, erection and best firing sites, Dornberger offering thirty of his men to help with the tests. The rocket troops assisting in the exercise who formed into the *Altenwalde Versuchskommando (AVKO)*, a military style unit under the command of Lieutenant Colonel Weber, one-time commander of the very successful Training and Experimental Battery 444, included everyone, civilian and military, involved in the final preparations – and the launches themselves; all had significant operational experience with V2s in the field and would add logistical support. For the purpose of the exercise, and for some rocket work thereafter, some who were already in US custody were lent to the British. Other prominent Germans who contributed to BACKFIRE were Kurt Debus, who had been responsible for Peenemünde's Test Stand VII, Hans Fichtner and Al Zeiler, while British rocket specialists would be on hand to witness the preparatory work and the firings. Two thousand Canadian engineers, supplemented by a force of British soldiers, took three weeks to refurbish existing facilities and build special equipment for the trials, which included a giant proofing tower, a vertical structure for testing the rockets in their launch position, constructed from parts of a redundant Bailey bridge. The majority of the

British, American and French officers witness the live firing of a V2 from the Cuxhaven Weapons Range during the British Operation BACKFIRE, in September 1945, many German specialists on the weapon assisting on site. (Author, Courtesy HTM Peenemünde)

British weapons specialists trace the launch of a V2 during Operation BACKFIRE.
(Author, Courtesy HTM Peenemünde)

rocket technicians and their assistants arrived at Altenwalde on 22 July
where they were split into two groups and interrogated, a final group
joining them in the second week of August.

Initially, there was some concern that the Germans intended to assist
in the British trials might not be welcomed by those who had been on the
receiving end of the V2 attacks but this proved to be ill-founded. Likewise,
those Germans who were already in US custody in Bavaria, and who had
been hoping for free passage to a new life in America, were very reluctant to
be drafted to support BACKFIRE. However, they were somewhat consoled
by the treatment they received from the British, additional pay, special
rations, normal working hours in their specialisation, often with old friends,
while enjoying recreational activities and plenty of freedom to roam in the
local area.

From the eight V2s available, (some of these had been secreted away from
Nordhausen by the British before the Americans arrived, others were found
in railway wagons abandoned in Jerxheim and Lesse, North Germany) five
were prepared for the trials. Long and intensive searches gradually revealed

the necessary support equipment, found hidden away in the British zone of occupation around Celle, Fallingbostel and Lisse, much of it needing repair and refurbishment. Again, after much searching, a factory at Fassburg was re-opened to produce liquid oxygen, 70 tons of ethyl-alcohol was found on a train near Nordhausen and a stock of hydrogen-peroxide was found in Kiel. By mid-August the British had assembled and organised all the elements required for the two phases of BACKFIRE. Phase One dealt with the assembly of the rockets and all the ancillary equipment, Phase Two the final preparations, launches and behaviour of the rockets in flight. The German support was divided into two groups; the *AVKO* in Camp A, while a separate entity comprising twenty of von Braun's senior civilian staff made responsible for recording every aspect of the trials were lodged in Camp C. In addition to the Canadian contingent, some 150 scientists, 100 rocket troops and a working party of 600 PoWs were involved, and all was set for the trials to begin by the middle of September 1945.

The first launch, scheduled for 27 September 1945, was postponed because of bad weather and on 1 October two more attempts failed, due to ignition faults. However, at 14.41 on a bright and clear 2 October, everything worked perfectly, bringing plaudits all round; the rocket reached a height of 23, 000 feet and a distance of 154 miles. Just after the second launch, on 4 October, the engine failed but, on 15 October, a third launch at 15.06, before a large number of British, American, Russian and French spectators, was successful, climbing to 21,000 feet and landing, as planned, 144 miles down the range.

Despite the small number of launches, Operation BACKFIRE was considered to have been a great success – and very well worthwhile in the context of future research into stratospheric, supersonic rocketry. The evaluation had proved more difficult to stage than had been anticipated, *inter alia* heaping great credit upon the *Wehrmacht's* rocket troops who had once contributed their best under threat from the air at all times in the field, during the confusion and turbulence of war, and had now done so again in the relatively benign environment of peace.

Following the operation those of von Braun's team of specialists who had been detached from Bavaria were returned there, to be accommodated at a disused *Wehrmacht* barracks at Landshut, known as Camp Overcast, the British having failed to persuade the Americans to let them keep some of the rocketeers for their own purposes. At Camp Overcast, 150 of the scientists and technicians were offered five-year contracts to work for the US Army in the USA, their families looked after at Camp Overcast until arrangements could be made for them to be accommodated in America. This was the beginning of Operation OVERCAST, later Operation PAPERCLIP, in which a chosen few were moved to the Aberdeen Proving Ground, Maryland, via New York, in September 1945, while others from Peenemünde were given employment, initially at Fort Bliss, Texas, pending a more permanent home for all the Germans at White Sands, New Mexico, where, in April 1946, the first of some sixty V2s taken from Mittelwald, re-christened 'Bumper' was launched. Many rockets based on V2 technology followed, in many different configurations. The Americans had rich pickings and they did not delay putting their new acquisitions to work.

Although the British had failed to recruit some of German rocket scientists they wanted, they did get the service of others, employing them at the Royal Aircraft Establishments at Westcott and Farnborough where they made significant contributions out of all proportion to their numbers. The V2s they had acquired also provided the model for a British-designed equivalent, which incorporated a small cabin for training an astronaut – but nothing came of it.

Chapter 12

The Reckoning

Statistics on the V1 and V2 offensive against Britain and targets on the continent, primarily Antwerp and Liege, vary considerably between the sources but the figures below give some idea of the dimension of the *Vergeltungswaffen* offensive and what the recipients of these terror weapons had to endure during the nine-month campaign. The German people suffered too, not only from accidents in the missiles' development and production, but also from errant missiles on the front line. Then there were the thousands of foreign labourers and PoWs, who endured unspeakable deprivations, starvation and retribution, before many of them succumbed to a blessed death, particularly at Peenemünde, Mittelwerk, and in building the massive launch sites in the Pas de Calais.

One source has it that Wachtel's *Flak Regiment 155(W)* fired a total of 12,263 V1s, of which 9,521 targeted England, 5,672 crossed the coast and 2,340 reached Greater London, killing some 5,500 and seriously injuring 17,000. The worst V1 incident was at New Cross on 25 November 1944, when 168 people were killed and 121 injured, while those that hit the borough of Croydon destroyed 110,000 houses and damaged another 1,500,000, while 500 people were killed by the flying bombs elsewhere in England. Antwerp and Liège were the primary targets for the 2,448 V1s launched on the continent, causing an enormous number of casualties among the residents and transient Allied troops.

Of the 5,200 V2s built, only 3,000 were launched operationally, 1,115 against England, of which 517 hit London, killing 2,754 Londoners and seriously injuring 6,523, while 537 landed elsewhere in Britain, ended up in the North Sea, burst prematurely or broke up in the air. Overall, the V-weapons destroyed 107,000 houses in Britain, and damaged a further 1,500,000. Another 1,664 V2s were fired at Antwerp, killing 1,736 and injuring 4,500, the worst incident being on 16 December 1944, when 567 were killed and 291 injured with a direct hit on the Rex Cinema. France was the target for seventy-six V2s, The Netherlands nineteen and Germany eleven. A total of 12,000 PoWs and slave labourers were

188

thought to have died in the production of the two weapons at Peenemünde and Mittelwerk.

However, statistics alone do not tell the whole story of expensive time delays, procrastination and vacillation within the respective German and British hierarchies, of wasted effort, conflicting political and personal agendas, all combining to reduce the impact of the new weapons on the course of the war – and the effectiveness of the Allied defences against them. Many lessons were also learned, or re-learned on both sides, and it is worth summarising some of the more obvious here.

In attempting to supplement their armoury of long-range artillery with flying bombs and rockets, the Germans were able to circumvent some of the main constraints of the 1919 Treaty of Versailles, *inter alia* putting themselves way ahead of any other nation in guided-weapon technology and thus able to inflict a heavy blow on the Allies in England and on the continent. However, they failed to capitalise fully on their potential. At least in the early years it was von Braun who persuaded Hitler that the A4 (V2) was worth pursuing, and kept him updated with every optimistic development. Similarly, the Luftwaffe was playing catch-up with the FZG-76/Fi 103 (V1) flying bomb, without the official backing it needed from Erhard Milch, second in command of the air force, who paid only lip service to the project (Chapter Three). Attitudes changed when it seemed that both weapons could be effective additions to the arsenal, and Heinrich Himmler himself began taking a keen interest when it seemed that both missiles were about to materialise. Himmler had no interest in the missiles *per se,* in their quality control, improvements in guidance or terminal accuracy, only in the number of missiles he could bring under command and when, believing that ownership of the two programmes would bring additional power to his SS. Indeed, his utter contempt for the project scientists and engineers was very evident when, in March 1944, he had von Braun, Klaus Riedel and Helmut Gröttrup arrested on trumped-up charges (Chapter Three), presumably thinking that it would not be difficult to replace them. Dornberger and Speer knew better and pleaded successfully for their release to enable them continue their unique contributions. More delays were attributed to Himmler in the wake of Operation HYDRA when he insisted that all work in progress must be moved from Peenemünde to the relative safety of Mittelwerk, at a particularly crucial time for the A4/V2, when the Baltic site was on the point of completing vital work there. He also claimed that only complete control by his SS could weed out agents and spies embedded in the foreign workforce and prevent further leaks on the classified work which were believed to be helping the Allies.

Above all, however, there were the delays caused by Hitler blowing hot and cold over the V-weapons, and more specifically on the provision of a facility at Peenemünde to generate A4s for pre-production trials, the Führer only becoming more decisive in their favour when he realised that they offered the only means of retaliating in kind for the Allies' heavy bombing of German cities. Then, having eventually given his backing, Hitler would not hear of any obstacle to the production of the missiles, brushing aside von Braun's warning that the A4 was meant to be a test vehicle, optimised for trials only, not as an operational weapon – and von Braun was right. Early production V2s were found to have many defects, including disintegration before impact, leading to more delays as many hundreds of modifications had to be incorporated in the field. Haste here had been a false economy.

In addition to the lack of official encouragement in the right quarters, competition for critical resources, the raw materials, skills and equipment needed for the evolutionary weapons, delayed the 'in-service' dates of both missiles. For instance, compromises had to be accepted in the V2 guidance system, because the Kreiselgeräte company was unable to undertake a long run of the Sg 66 system, due to other demands on the firm. Also, with an initial paucity of equipment needed to complete the production of the V2s at MIttelwerk, the incomplete missiles had to be transported to Berlin to have their electrical systems added. Building a rocket in this way took eleven months, five of which were consumed remedying defects encountered during the trials at Blizna. Even when the campaign of these ill-proven weapons got into its stride, internal tensions and inter-service rivalries at all levels held back technical improvements and tactical deployments far more than any Allied actions against them. Also, the fierce competition between the respective protagonists of the flying bomb and the rocket to get their missiles to the front line first was driven more by the prestige it could bestow than military imperatives, so there was little if any cross-flow of information or co-operation between the two project teams, all of which was again counter-protective, and, once operational, it was the respective launch rates which mattered. On the front line and in the rear areas, further modifications, running repairs and improvisation were the order of the day, with little time or expertise remaining to improve performance. One exception was the introduction of lightweight V1s, given wooden wings and nose, and a smaller warhead to allow more fuel for greater range, but this came too late to Influence the course of the war. Crucially, the guidance system was never improved, but shortening the range of the flying bombs from their launch sites to continental targets did improve their accuracy.

THE RECKONING

Those who argued that the resources allotted to the V-weapons could have been better spent on manned aircraft production may not have been aware that, from the beginning in 1943, the Luftwaffe had all the material resources it needed for aircraft production although supplies of aviation fuel to the front line was fast becoming inadequate; the main problem was a dire shortage of pilots, especially experienced pilots. In fact, in 1944, the German aircraft industry produced more fighters than the Luftwaffe could man despite many of its skilled mechanics being drafted into the ground defence force. Given that the Luftwaffe's twin-engine bombers were obsolescent, and that it had no heavy bombers, the V1s and V2s were the only strike assets available, so they became Hitler's darlings of the time.

Much time was wasted in building Hitler's initial preference for huge concrete launch sites for the V2s in France, and many of the V1 static ski sites, in the obvious path of an inevitable Allied invasion; the thousands of men involved and the supporting logistics would have been better employed elsewhere. From the German standpoint, the best that can be said of the static sites, particularly those which acted as decoys, with skeleton manning and cosmetic repairs, is that they diverted a great deal of Allied air effort away from other more profitable targets. Bombing the huge, semi-underground reinforced-concrete launch sites in France (Watten, Wizernes, Siracourt and Mimoyecques), before their completion may have been necessary, but it certainly found no favour with the chiefs of Bomber Command and the USAAF's 8th Air Force. They claimed that their best contribution to CROSSBOW was to continue bombing the German heartland, with the target list including those industries involved in the production of the two missiles. Be that as it may, the heavy bombers were said to have flown nearly 70,000 sorties and dropped 122,000 tons of bombs on CROSSBOW targets with no little objective evidence of their success. However, the 'law of unintended consequences' did play its part here, when the bombing of bunker and ski sites drove the Germans into dispersing their missile launch sites tactically. Thereafter, the Allies had to mount countless reconnaissance sorties, to seek out these elusive, fleeting sites for the fighter-bombers to follow, often to no avail and always at risk from increasingly effective German AA. Additional resources also had to be found to counter the V1s air-launched over the North Sea and those targeting the logistics centres at Antwerp and Liège, while the port at Ghent had to be activated to back up Antwerp, given the German successes with the V-weapons there.

The old adage that 'time spent in reconnaissance is never wasted', was certainly true in Operation CROSSBOW but only when good visual reports and photographs were subjected to expert scrutiny and acted on in time. There is good evidence that the photographic interpreters (PIs) at the Medmenham CIU served the Allies well but such intelligence as they produced, even that which was well validated, was not always used expeditiously, or to best effect, in necessarily precise mission planning, weapons/target matching and employment to be carried out against the likely enemy activity and weather in the operating area. This often resulted in many sorties having to be aborted, wasted effort or unnecessary collateral damage, the raids against Peenemünde in August 1943, and that against the Haagse Bos in March 1944, providing examples of this (Chapter Eight). In the former PR had revealed the most important target elements at Peenemünde but poor bombing resulted in the death of only one of the key scientists, Dr Thiel, at a cost of forty-one RAF bombers and their crews, and the loss of several important informants who were killed when the PoW/foreign workers' sleeping quarters were destroyed. Failure to rectify this mistake with a second attempt was, in hindsight, another major blunder, allowing valuable work at Peenemünde to continue almost unhindered from the air until the Russians were on the doorstep. In the latter case, the raid against the Haagse Bos, inadequate mission preparation and inaccurate bombing, arguably employing unsuitable assets, caused the deaths of some 500 Dutch civilians and the total destruction of Bezuidenhout.

The author, a one-time fighter-bomber/tactical reconnaissance pilot himself, and later a battle manager in NATO, is anxious not to lay blame for some lack of definitive success in this air war against the V1s and V2s, particularly in seeking out and destroying such obscure ground targets without the sophisticated aids to navigation and weapons delivery, and with none of the precision-guided weapons available today. He fully recognises the enormous difficulties faced by the planners in prioritising targets in a fast-moving situation, the co-ordination of inter-dependent forces and the many agencies involved in the multiple, conflicting tasks they faced in 1944/45 – so often in the necessary haste and fog of war. Despite the pre-eminence of the Allies, they too faced a paucity of resources, especially when the demands of the impending invasion competed with those of CROSSBOW at critical times in 1944.

To their credit, the Allied tactical air forces soon realised that, once found, the elusive V2 and 'modified' V1 sites had to be reported or attacked without delay, before they 'went to ground' or were moved on. This was no easy task, either requiring suitably equipped and armed fighter-bombers to be already airborne in the area awaiting such tasks, held on the ground at immediate readiness close to the action, or by tasking armed reconnaissance sorties on *ad hoc* 'seek and strike' sorties (Chapter Eight). Attempts to employ medium bombers against these targets were short lived; invariably they were too late and too inaccurate.

It is perhaps understandable that, with the Germans in full retreat in the face of the Allied forces in the west, targeting and weapons employment within and between the two missile camps, the army artillery and Luftwaffe, did not follow the generally accepted principles of war to the letter – or indeed in some cases at all. Take into account, too, the fact that *SS-Obergruppenführer* Hans Kammler and his staff, ultimately in full control of the V1s and V2, had no previous experience of missile operations and that he was interested only in symbolism reflected in the number of weapons launched, and at what rate, so that the collective offensive/defensive forces were not employed to best effect. For instance, had the principle of 'concentration of force' been achieved by synchronising and co-ordinating attacks by the missiles, heavy artillery and air forces, mounted from different directions to thin out the defences more, this could have caused even greater damage in Antwerp port, further demoralising the stevedores, slowing the outflow of men and materials and thus the advance of the Allies across Europe.

Moreover, both weapons were frittered away against targets of no real military consequence, or, given their known inaccuracies, had little chance of succeeding in their purpose. So it was that several towns in Belgium were targeted with too few missiles to achieve significant success in slowing the Allied advance, while others were aimed, surely more in hope than expectation, at the crucial Remagen bridge over the Rhine, leaving only twenty-two of the 150 available at that time to be launched at London – this only escaping the Führer's wrath because of the visibly high launch rate. It was to the Allies' good fortune that failures of this kind saved the three primary city targets (London, Antwerp and Liège) from greater devastation. In fact, the records suggest that there was little or no discussion on target priorities, or weapons' co-ordination in the final stages of the war, both Kammler and Wechtel sensibly abiding by Hitler's will to target London, if too late to have any great effect. Nor does there seem to have been any analysis of weapons results, most of the German agents in London having been 'turned' (Chapter Four); and no evidence has been found that any agents they might have had in Belgium provided the information on 'fall of shot' necessary for the aiming points in Antwerp to be adjusted.

While the Allied offensive forces experienced great difficulties finding and suppressing the elusive missile targets on the continent, the active and passive defences against the V1 in England were having greater success. Following the inevitable complaints from the airmen that the gunners either lacked the necessary aircraft recognition skills or were a little too 'trigger-happy', and from the gunners that the airmen were violating their gun defended areas, Air Marshal Sir Roderick Hill and Lieutenant General Sir Frederick Pile re-organised their fighters and guns to give the best possible chance of avoiding 'blue-on-blue' engagements and downing the flying bombs (Chapter Six). A similar situation existed in the air defence of Antwerp where the same invaluable lessons were learned in inter-service cooperation. In neither case, however, were they successful enough, the ultimate defence against the V1s and V2s coming only with the occupation of all the missile launch sites; until then massive resources had to be diverted to counter the V1s. The V2s could not, of course, be intercepted in the air; they had to be destroyed on the ground.

Attempts to compare the accuracy and effectiveness of the unguided 'dumb' bombs dropped from aircraft by either side during the war with those achieved by the V1 and V2 are likely to be inconclusive, given the widely varying statistics available, all of which depended on the timing and circumstances in which they were derived, anecdotal stories suffering likewise – and often with emotions added. The author, who lived in the London suburbs throughout the Blitz of 1940/41, witnessed a very large number of bombs falling in open countryside, some 15 miles or more from the centre of London and with no significant military or industrial target in the area. The Allies suffered too from poor bombing accuracies, various estimates suggesting that, particularly in the early years of the war and at night, the RAF sometimes missed its targets by as much as five to nine miles and even a great deal more, even the much revered Pathfinders of later years being known to get it wrong (vide Operation HYDRA, Chapter Eight). The Americans, flying in daylight, using their excellent Norden bombsights, did better, but all the Allied bomber fleets suffered very heavy losses from the formidable German defences, on many occasions having to jettison their bombs or abort their sorties due to battle damage or bad weather – problems which did not affect the German missiles. In summary, the immature V-weapons were less accurate than the bomber crews could achieve, particularly with their state-of-the-art bombing equipment in 1944/45 but, had the V-weapons been perfected before use, it might have been a very different story.

Turning to a comparison of destructive powers, there was no variation in the warheads of the V1 (1,870lb Amatol) and V2 (2,000lb Amatol), other than a slight reduction in the updated V1's warhead to allow more fuel to give greater range, whereas the manned bombers and fighter-bombers, could be fitted with a wide variety of weapons, of different yields, up to the 20,000lb Grand Slam bombs delivered only by RAF Lancasters. The destructive effects of the V-weapons then depended on three self-explanatory variables, penetration, blast and fragmentation, and they in turn depended on the speed and angle at which they struck their targets. In the case of the V1s these variables were unpredictable, the bomb having dived from a relatively low height band of 2,000 to 6,000feet, limiting its maximum penetration. Indeed the author remembers some V1s hitting from a very shallow glide, with minimum penetration but maximum blast and fragmentation, whereas the V2s would invariably hit the ground vertically, at supersonic speeds, resulting in maximum penetration but less widespread blast and fragmentation. The terminal speeds and strike angles could, to a certain extent, be determined by the tactics employed by the delivery aircraft.

So much for some (but not all) technical comparisons but, for any debate on overall 'cost-effectiveness' of the two V-missiles *vis a vis* the manned bomber, it is vital to view them in the circumstances at the time. To claim that because the entire tonnage of explosives delivered by the V2s did not amount to that dropped in a single thousand-bomber raid on Germany rendered the German rocket offensive a gross waste of money would be a calumny. In the nine-month timeframe of V1 and V2 operations (June 1944-March 1945), when the Germans had their 'backs to the wall', with only obsolescent twin-engine aircraft and no heavy bombers, they had no means of striking back other than with these new weapons and it cannot be denied that these caused a great deal of disruption to the Allied war plans, let alone the impact they had on morale, at home and on the continent. The Allies had little alternative but to continue committing much of their air power against the main bunkers and highly elusive launch sites in the Pas de Calais, the complex supply system, and perhaps the environs to the vital Middelwerk plant – more in hope than expectation of success.

On face value, some cost comparisons can be very persuasive until they are scrutinised closely and qualified, when they may become meaningless. For instance, the total financial cost of the Peenemünde operation has been assessed at four times that of the Manhattan Atomic Project, which produced the atomic bomb but, of course, there were very different objectives here, in different times and in different circumstances; this would not be a fair, like-for-like comparison. For a realistic comparison, manned bomber operations must include the costs of aircraft development and production, the running costs of the factories, the construction and maintenance of huge airfields and other support facilities, all very vulnerable to air attack. Then there were the recurring costs of aircrew training and replacements for those lost in action to increasingly effective air defences, or for other reasons, all adding to the enormous costs of consumables, such as fuel and weapons. Similar costs applied to the development and testing of the V-weapons, but the only partially successful raids on Peenemünde drove production deep underground at Mittelwerk, immune from Allied 'dumb' bombs, leaving only a scattering of component factories prey to Allied bombs. Also, the operating costs of the missiles were relatively low, since they required no expensive airfields from which to operate. The text above only touches on the myriad, contentious arguments on the cost comparisons of the main offensive weapons systems in the latter stages of the war and draws no conclusions. The jury is still out.

What befell the main players on the two sides? Regardless of the subjective and objective judgements on their strengths and limitations during the *Vergeltungswaffen* campaign, many stalwarts continued to make their mark on history thereafter, but had they learned from their experiences of the potential of long-range missiles and how best to counter them? The debate on the possibility of missile attacks on Britain may have begun, in slow time, early in the war, admittedly with fragmented, inconclusive evidence on the possibilities and nature of such threats, but it did not get underway in earnest until 1943(Chapter Four). By then, for those who wish to see it, there was plenty of evidence that the Allies should be concerned. Churchill and R.V. Jones were much concerned, but the Chief Scientific Adviser, Lord Cherwell, was not.

The driving force behind the CROSSBOW campaign, Prime Minister Churchill, fell from political grace in the 1945 election, only to rise again in 1951, and his story needs no rehearsal. The controversial Lord Cherwell, famous for his early disbelief in the German missiles and his sometimes rash predictions, was made Paymaster General for a second time in 1951 and given a seat in the Cabinet before becoming Viscount Cherwell of Oxford in 1956, a year before his death at the age of 71. Duncan Sandys, Churchill's son-in-law, who was frequently at loggerheads with others in the Crossbow Committee, also lost his seat in Parliament in 1945, but returned as a conservative MP thereafter, most prominently as the Minister of Defence in the mid-1950s when, to almost universal dismay, he reduced RAF fighter numbers to a token force in favour of guided missiles. He was elevated to the peerage, as Baron Duncan Sandys, in 1974. R.V. Jones was appointed CB in 1946 in recognition of his contribution to science and given a Chair at Aberdeen University; he became a Fellow of the Royal Society in 1965 and was appointed Companion of Honour in 1994. He died in 1997.

It is a strange irony that the fortunes of war sometimes favour the losers, a point well proven in the case of the chief protagonists of the *Vergeltungswaffen,* Wernher von Braun and Walter Dornberger, the victors wisely foreseeing their inestimable value in the future of rocket science. Both claimed to have predicted defeat in 1944 when they attempted, covertly, to negotiate terms with the US General Electric Company through the German Embassy in Lisbon, which might have got them to America long before the end of the war. Both von Braun and Dornberger pleaded that the original driving force behind their rocket initiatives was the conquest of space but that they had no alternative, given the political and military pressures of the 1930s, but to defer to the Nazis and the imperatives of war – as a means to an end. One Jewish comedian modified the name of a film which featured von Braun, *I Aim at The Stars* to *I Aim at The Stars, but Sometimes I hit London* (Chapter Two). In the end, neither was accused of war crimes and did not undergo the sometimes humiliating interrogations which awaited many of their colleagues, the Allies, particularly the Americans, being more interested in them for their potential. So it was that they were separated from their main party of Peenemünde weaponeers at Oberjoch in early May 1945 and taken to Garmisch-Partenkirchen to be interviewed by Dr Richard Porter, a systems engineer for the American General Electric Company. However, as a gesture to the British, and at the instigation of London's MI14, it was agreed that von Braun could spend seven days in London to be interviewed primarily by Sir Alwyn Crow at the Ministry of Supply. He and Dornberger also contributed to the British Operation BACKFIRE (Chapter Eleven), the latter remaining with the British for a further two years before he too ended up in America, as an employee of the Bell Aircraft Company. Unrepentant, von Braun continued to laugh his way to the bank as he helped America with the space race and their successful effort to put their man on the moon with the giant Saturn V booster rocket in July 1969. Von Braun died in 1977, aged 65.

No such good fortune awaited the dynamic and ruthless *SS-Obergruppenführer* Hans Kammler. On the evidence of his driver, *Oberscharführer* Kurt Preuk, he had escaped to Prague where he had taken cyanide and was buried there on 9 May 1944. Others believed that he shot himself, had himself shot, moved to live in America – or on the moon!

Wolfgang Wetzling, who carried out Kammler's orders to exterminate those found cooking chickens in the woods around Warstein, was captured, found guilty of his crimes and imprisoned for life.

Those less in the limelight, the Luftwaffe men who produced and operated the V1 flying bomb, were not in great demand, and the Allies showed no interest in bringing the chief operator, Max Wachtel, alias '*Oberst* Wolf', to trial (Chapter Four); could he indeed be called a war criminal? Little seems to be known about his ultimate fate, other than in a story that he refused to discuss his extensive knowledge of the V1 and its operation with the Allies unless and until they had found one Isabelle de Goy. This they did, for the two to marry in 1947, after which it is said he became manager of Hamburg International Airport.

One of the salient principles of war is 'Maintenance of morale', of the troops involved and of the civilians affected, and in this the V-weapons played an important part on both sides. Throughout the war Joseph Goebbels developed a highly efficient Ministry of Public Enlightenment and Propaganda, which broadcast continuously to the German masses, by which means many Germans came to believe that London was being 'pulverised' under a hail of V1s and V2s, with thousands fleeing the capital in panic, and by claims that these new weapons would swing the war in their favour. To them, their V-weapons were worth every *pfennig* (penny). Not forgetting the British, Goebbels arranged for the British traitor William Joyce (Lord Haw-Haw) to broadcast a very different version of the war news to that given by the BBC and there is no doubt that the mystique and the 'fear factor' attached to the V1 and V2 had an adverse effect on a tired nation's productivity and morale.

For them, there lurked a crucial question: why would the Germans spend so much effort on the missiles unless the warheads were going to carry something more sinister than explosives, perhaps a chemical or biological agent? It was certainly to mankind's benefit generally that they did not, and that the German scientists did not expend their undoubted talents on splitting the atom, or indeed that the hierarchy did not take the simpler expedient of giving the development of the V-weapons greater momentum. Had they done so, and the missiles had become operational six months earlier, the huge assembly areas in England and ultimate destinations of the Allied invasion forces might have come under a devastating hail of flying bombs and rockets. Could such a prospect have resulted in the postponement or cancellation of the invasion or its failure ashore – or even worse? Who knows?

Chapter 13

Requiem

Thousands of monuments litter continental Europe and the United Kingdom, bearing testimony to the tragedies of the Second World War generally and in the particular. Specifically, the new mode of warfare unleashed by Germany in the dying months of war, involving the innovative stratospheric rocket and flying bomb, gave rise to a spate of memorials, the number, of course, being too great to list here. However, a small sample should suffice to illustrate the consciousness and, in some cases the conscience of the perpetrators, of the twin campaign which killed so many in the trials, construction, deployments and launch of these new weapons of war, leaving death, destruction and misery in their paths. This requiem is limited primarily to the birthplace of the *Vergeltungswaffen,* Peenemünde, the main production centre at Mittelbau Dora, the first V1 launch area against England, in the Pas de Calais, The Hague and those who suffered in and around London, each having its own agonising tale to tell.

Let these photographs be a reminder.

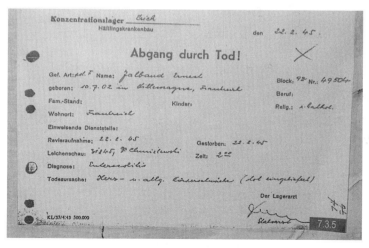

A reminder of the extraordinary detail in which the Germans recorded the PoWs and slave labourers. (Author, Courtesy HTM Peenemünde)

Above: This evocative mural commemorates the mass grave of slave labourers and PoWs, many clearly executed, found at Karlshagen and reburied in 1968. (Author)

Left: Known only to God – the author kneels before a memorial to 213 foreign workers at Peenemünde. (Author)

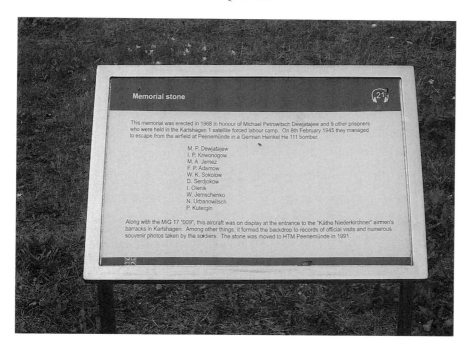

Above: Tribute to a Russian pilot, Lieutenant M.D. Demjatejew, a PoW at Peenemünde, who stole a Luftwaffe Heinkel 111 bomber from the airfield and escaped back to Russian with nine fellow PoWs. (Author, Courtesy HTM Peenemünde)

Right: A monument to Russian PoWs buried in the Peenemünde forest, identified by Lieutenant Demjatejew. (Author, Courtesy HTM Peenemünde)

This plaque at Siracourt, Pas de Calais, laid by French and Russian Second World War veterans, remembers the Soviet PoWs who suffered and died building the V1 launch site there in 1944. (Author)

These stones commemorate the deaths of 2,000 service personnel and civilians killed in the RAF and USAAF raids on Peenemünde in 1943 and 1944. (Author)

This stone, in the rocket trials area at Peenemünde, remembers the first A4 (V2s) fired there in 1943. (Author)

As the number of deaths resulting from the brutal treatment of the PoWs and slave labourers at Mittelbau-Dora rose, so did tell-tale smoke from the crematorium. (Author, Courtesy Mittelbau)

This classic photograph, taken by a US Army photographer at the SS Boelcke Barracks, Nordhausen, on 11 April 1945, encapsulates the horror of war, the dead, dying and horribly emaciated bodies of the Mittelwerk PoWs and slave labourers attributed to Nazi brutality but also to the RAF raids on the town on the nights of 3-5 April. (Author's Collection)

This tablet, on a wall in Sloan Square, London, remembers the deaths of 76 US Army servicemen and three civilians caused by a V1 on 3 July 1944. (Author)

Built into the foundations are the remains

of some two thousand memorials

damaged beyond repair

when the chapel was destroyed

on 18ᵗʰ June 1944.

Above: War takes its toll on heritage, as this plaque in the Guards Chapel testifies. (Author, Courtesy The Guards Chapel)

Right: The altar, silver cross and six candles remained in place when a V1 shattered the remainder of the Guards Chapel in London on 18 June 1944. (Author, Courtesy The Guards Chapel)

Above: A memorial stone, deep underground, remembers the RAF airmen lost in raids against Mimoyecques. (Author, Courtesy Mimoyecques)

Left: A memorial to Joe Kennedy Jr in the Mimoyecques caves. (Author Courtesy Mimoyecques)

An English Heritage Blue Plaque marks the spot where the first V1 to land in London struck Grove Road, Bethnal Green, on 13 June 1944, killing 6 and injuring 30. (Author)

The V2 which landed on crowded shops in Lewisham on 25 November 1944 killed 168 people and injured many others is marked by this plaque. (Author)

207

A stone commemorates all those who suffered from the V2 attacks in the Chiswick and Brentford area, the first in London having struck Chiswick on 8 September 1944. (Author)

Epilogue

In an amazing feat of innovation, improvisation and determination, leading to remarkable scientific achievements in the late 1930s and early 1940s, Nazi Germany led the world in rocket and flying-bomb technology, far ahead of any other country. That they did so, with so little initial reaction in Britain, was due in part to the conviction among a few eminent scientists, especially Frederick Lindemann (later Lord Cherwell), that such evidence as emerged, at first in snippets but later in an veritable avalanche, had been 'planted' or was sheer propaganda. They also asked how, if Britain had not achieved any real success with a rocket, necessarily powered by liquid fuel to give it the range to reach London, could the Germans have done so? There was scepticism, too, in Germany. Despite strenuous efforts on the part of the main protagonists of the stratospheric, supersonic rocket, (Wernher von Braun and Walter Dornberger), some within the German political and military establishments, including the Führer, were slow to grasp the war-fighting potential of the two missiles. This scepticism, on both sides, would influence the in-service dates and effectiveness of these weapons, and the defences against them.

The V-weapons may not have achieved what the Führer and many others in the Third Reich had hoped for, and even expected, that of winning the war for them 'in the final innings', but it would be a calumny to see them as 'complete failures', as several authors have claimed. True, they were inaccurate, had insufficient range, their warheads were too small and, above all, they came too late to alter the course of the war. They may not have 'terrorised' most Londoners, or prevented supplies passing through Antwerp or Liège, but for a variety of reasons they had proved more than a nuisance to the Allies. The endless, often contentious, debates which raged in London alone on the likelihood of rocket and/or flying-bomb attacks on the Allies, and what defensive measures might be put in place against such exigencies, absorbed great minds and consumed valuable time at a critical stage in the war. Before and during the V-weapons campaign the Allies were forced to commit a great deal of the manpower and material originally earmarked for OVERLORD and the strategic bombing of Germany, to CROSSBOW targets, many of which were in friendly countries such as France, Belgium and Holland, which pleased the Führer, who said 'every bomb dropped (by the Allies) on a CROSSBOW target was one less on the German heartland'. So it was that the V-weapons contributed to Germany's war effort in many ways.

In the Allied camp, it had been taken for granted that the Germans would lose the war before the V1s and V2s took to the skies, and throughout their short operational life there remained no doubt that they would, but they did influence Allied plans and tie up thousands of Allied aircraft, AA, men and women in the last year of the war, thereby delaying their advance through Europe, and thus the end of the war. Typically, the need to cut off and suppress the missile launch sites proliferating in west Holland in the summer of 1944 caused Eisenhower and Montgomery to change their plans for crossing the Rhine from the ideal flatlands west of Wesel, to the more hazardous areas around Arnhem, with disastrous results for Operation MARKET GARDEN.

Why did the Germans continue to pour precious resources, in manpower and material, into their production and delivery of the V1s and V2s at the expense of the defensive measures they so urgently needed to stem the Allies' advance towards Nazi Germany, and to counter the heavy bomber raids on their cities? Did the Germans really believe Joseph Goebbels' very persuasive propaganda that these ill-proven missiles would turn the tide of war in their favour, or could there have been a more sinister possibility, certainly postulated in London, that the missiles were about to be re-equipped with chemical, biological – or even nuclear warheads?

It could have been so much worse for the Allies. The bombardment of London made no military sense, it was simply Hitler's obsession with retaliation in kind for the heavy air raids on German cities. Had the missiles been concentrated on the invasion assembly areas, the embarkation ports and disembarkation beaches, where military men and equipment were massed together in highly lucrative targets, the results could have been catastrophic for the Allies. Eisenhower is known to have suggested that this might have led to the postponement, even cancellation of Operation OVERLORD.

I find no good reason to disbelieve Wernher von Braun's claim that he, his mentors and cohorts approached the new world of supersonic, stratospheric rocketry primarily to explore the mysteries of space but that, in the circumstances at the time, they had no sensible alternative but to cede to Nazi demands for military applications. Of course there is some evidence, albeit perhaps difficult to prove, that von Braun himself, and others in his team, were complicit to some extent in war crimes, but given their inherent value to the Allies, pragmatism prevailed. So it was that their post-war employment with the Allies, mainly with the Americans but to a lesser extent the Russians and the British, made good use of their hard-earned expertise in rocket and flying-bomb technology to help put a man on the moon, while developing future weapons of war. Perhaps the world should be grateful that dedication to these weapons diverted great scientific and technical minds away from early interest in nuclear research.

Looking at the war as a whole, those who remember the death and devastation in London during the 1940 Blitz (and I was one), not to mention that wrought on Coventry, Bristol, Hull and other provincial towns in Britain, or the German brutality in occupied countries, could be puzzled by Germany's use of the word *Vergeltungswaffen,* meaning 'retaliation', to describe the indiscriminate employment of V-weapons. The Allies did at least attempt to bomb, with precision, specific military or industrial targets within urban conurbations, whereas the V-weapons were unashamedly 'area terror' weapons when hurled at London, Antwerp, Liège *et al. Verzweiflung,* meaning 'desperation', might have been a more appropriate term for the V-weapons.

However, my sister and I had no such lofty thoughts as we rowed on that peaceful lake in Epping Forest. For us, and for those not directly affected by these weapons, life went on very much as usual. It was, of course, very different for those who suffered directly in this 'last gasp' offensive; their pain, loss and anguish can only be imagined but at that late stage of the war I think it most unlikely that Herr Hitler's *Vergeltungswaffen* would have brought Great Britain to its knees.

There remains one unanswered question. What difference would the V1s and V2s have made to the outcome of the war had not the many, self-inflicted delays prevented the missiles from becoming more effective, achieving greater accuracies and arriving on the front line in greater numbers, say, one year, or even six months earlier.

We will never know.

Bibliography

Bowyer, Michael J.F., *2 Group RAF – A Complete History: 1936-1945* (Faber and Faber, London, 1974)

Brandon, Lewis, *Night Flyer* (Crécy Publishing, Manchester, 1961)

Campbell, Christy, *Target London – Under Attack from V-Weapons* (Abacus, London, 2012)

Collier, Basil, *The Battle of the V-Weapons* (The Elmfield Press, London, 1964

Cooksley, Peter, *Flying Bomb* (Robert Hale Ltd, London, 1979)

Heitmann, Jan, *The Peenemünde Rocket Centre* (Battle of Britain International Ltd, London, 1991)

Hogg, Ian V., *German Secret Weapons* (Greenhill Books, London, 1999)

Johnson, David, *V for Vengeance* (William Kimber & Co Ltd, London, 1981)

Joubert, Sir Philip, *Rocket* (Hutchinson & Co, London, 1957)

King, Benjamin, and Timothy Kutta, *Impact: The History of Germany's V Weapons in WW2* (Spellmount, Staplehurst, 1988)

Margry, Karel, The V-Weapons (Battle of Britain International Ltd, London, 1974)*, Nordhausen* (Battle of Britain International Ltd, London, 1998)

Ogleby, Bob, *Doodlebugs & Rockets – The Battle of the Flying Bombs*: Froglet Publications, Westerham, 1992)

Pallud, Jean Paul, *The V3 & V4* (Battle of Britain International Ltd, London, 2001)

Pile, General Sir Frederick, *Ack-Ack. Britain's Defence Against Air Attack During the Second World War* (Collins, London, 1949)

Richards, Denis & Hilary Saunders, *Royal Air Force 1939-1945, Vol 3* (HMSO, London, 1974)

Rooke, Peter, *Cheshunt at War* (np, 1989)

Simpson, Bill, *Spitfire Dive-Bombers Versus the V-2* (Pen & Sword Books, Barnsley, 2007)

Smith, Graham, *The Mighty Eighth* (Countryside Books, Newbury, 2001)

Index